IEA Health and Welfare Unit
Choice in Welfare Series No. 10

The Moral Foundations of Market Institutions

The Moral Foundations of Market Institutions

John Gray

Commentaries by
Chandran Kukathas
Patrick Minford
Raymond Plant

First published in 1992
by
The IEA Health and Welfare Unit
2 Lord North St
London SW1P 3LB

ISBN 0-255 36271-4

Typeset by the IEA Health and Welfare Unit
in Palatino 11 on 12 point
Printed in Great Britain by
Goron Pro-Print Co. Ltd
Churchill Industrial Estate, Lancing, West Sussex

Contents

Foreword

In *The Moral Foundations of Market Institutions*, John Gray, the distinguished Oxford philosopher, examines the moral legitimacy of the market economy. His contribution is particularly timely as leaders of the former East European communist states and the new republics of the erstwhile Soviet Union turn to the West for understanding of the elements which make possible a free society.

For John Gray, autonomy is one of the vital ingredients of individual well-being. When speaking of autonomy he does not mean to imply that individuals live without reference to others, on the contrary he stresses the debt each of us owes to past generations and to the shared institutions of a free society. He values the efficiency of markets as much as anyone and his chapter on 'The Epistemic Argument for the Market' is rich in insight, stressing not only the incentives for exertion and creativity provided by the market, but also its adaptation to the limits and dispersed nature of human knowledge. But it is not the efficiency of markets that appeals most to Gray. For him, the chief justification of a market economy is that it facilitates individual autonomy.

Because he puts autonomous choice at the centre of his thinking, Gray sees a wider role for government than that traditionally favoured by libertarians. The minimal state is not enough and government must take responsibility for ensuring that all individuals enjoy access to the means of choice. John Gray is conscious of the dangers in this view and takes pains to distance himself from egalitarians who want government not only to come to the aid of the weakest in society, but also to equalise everyone. Gray has no truck with redistribution, and his chapter on 'The Mirage of Egalitarianism' is a stinging rebuttal of the egalitarian approach.

Gray defends himself against critics who assert that government has a tendency inexorably to expand, by insisting that a welfare state offering entitlements to welfare services can be maintained if the rights are confined to 'basic needs'. According to Gray, such needs are not infinitely expanding but can be satisfied. They are, he says, 'satiable needs'.

Choice in Welfare No 10 also includes commentaries by three of John Gray's critics, Professor Patrick Minford from the University of Liverpool, Chandran Kukathas, currently at the University of New South Wales, and Professor Raymond Plant from the University of Southampton. Both Minford and Kukathas take issue with the claim, which is pivotal to Gray's argument, that needs are satiable. They doubt that some demands for state services can be satisfied, with health care out in front as the obvious case. Gray concedes that there is some truth in this claim but still insists that the demand for public services will not expand indefinitely.

Chandran Kukathas, author of a respected study of Hayek (*Hayek and Modern Liberalism*, Oxford University Press, 1989) challenges another of John Gray's central assumptions. He finds Gray's view of autonomy too materialistic, that is, too focused on spending power or 'resources'. Kukathas looks back to an earlier generation of classical liberals who put good character at the fore. They too respected autonomy, but they did not understand it in material terms. They would have agreed that it was better if people enjoyed the material options that prosperity makes possible, but the autonomy which they celebrated was more about an inner struggle to be a better person than exercising choices among consumer goods. As J.S. Mill remarked, 'The worth of a state, in the long run, is the worth of the individuals composing it'. Consequently, he thought that public institutions should foster good 'moral, intellectual and active' qualities such as the moral attributes of honesty and integrity; the intellectual qualities of open-mindedness and enthusiasm for learning; and the active qualities of courage, determination and willingness to help others.

Classical liberals would also have agreed that a society is to be judged by how well it cares for the weak and vulnerable, but the main measure of success was not the extent of the welfare state, but the degree to which individuals devoted their own time and energy through voluntary associations to the service of others.

In both the West and the former communist countries, thinking people are struggling to understand the ideal balance between the powers of government and the freedom of citizens, both as individuals and as participants in intermediate structures like the family, business corporations and voluntary associations of all types. John Gray's paper proposes a new balance which borrows from the classical liberal, conservative and social-democratic traditions of thought. The classical liberalism shines through in Gray's unequivocal commitment to individual freedom and diversity and consequent suspicion of state power; Gray's conservatism is reflected in his sense of history and the debt we owe to traditional culture and morals; and social-democratic influence is reflected in Gray's inclination to accord the state the supreme role in providing for those who, for whatever reason, do not prosper in a free society. Gray does say that he wants private remedies to be exhausted before the state steps in, but there is little such reluctance to employ the state's powers in the practical measures he recommends. In this latter respect, the debate continues.

But putting aside such differences of view, John Gray's paper can be strongly recommended as a powerful, scholarly analysis of the institutions which make freedom possible, and as a timely reminder that the ideal we pursue is not so much that of a 'free *market*' but a 'free *society*'.

David G. Green

The Authors

John Gray was educated at Exeter College, Oxford, where he read Philosophy, Politics and Economics and received his B.A., M.A., and D. Phil degrees. Since 1976 he has been a Fellow of Jesus College, Oxford. He has had numerous visiting appointments, including Professor of Government at Harvard University, Visiting Distinguished Professor in Philosophy at Bowling Green State University, Ohio, Visiting Professor in Law at Emory University in Atlanta, and Visiting Distinguished Professor in Political Economy at the Murphy Institute at Tulane University, New Orleans.

His books include: *Mill on Liberty: A Defence; Hayek on Liberty; Liberalism; Liberalisms: Essays on Political Philosophy; Post-Liberalism: Studies in Political Thought, (forthcoming)*. His monographs include: *Limited Government: A Positive Agenda*, IEA Hobart Paper 113; *A Conservative Disposition: Individualism, The Free Market and the Common Life*, Centre for Policy Studies, Winter Address, 1991; *The Strange Death of Perestroika: Causes and Consequences of the Soviet Coup*, European Security Study 13, Institute for European Defence and Strategic Studies; *Advertising Bans: Administrative Decisions or Matters of Principle?* Social Affairs Unit. He is currently engaged in writing a history of political thought.

Chandran Kukathas was born in Malaysia where he completed his primary education. He finished his schooling in Canberra before going on to take his first degree in History and Politics at the Australian National University. He taught at the Royal Military College, Canberra, Oxford University (where he completed a doctorate) and the Australian National University, before taking up his present position as Senior Lecturer in Politics at the Australian Defence Force Academy, part of the University of New South Wales.

He is the author of: *Hayek and Modern Liberalism*, Oxford University Press, 1989; *The Theory of Politics: An Australian Perspective*, with David Lovell and William Maley, Longman Cheshire 1990; and *Rawls: A Theory of Justice and Its Critics*, with Philip Pettit, Polity Press 1990; and has most recently co-edited with David Lovell and William Maley, *The Transition from*

Socialism: State and Civil Society in the USSR, Longman Cheshire, 1991.

Patrick Minford has been Edward Gonner Professor of Applied Economics at the University of Liverpool since 1976. Previously he held posts as the Economic Assistant to the Finance Director, Courtaulds Ltd.; Economics Adviser, Ministry of Finance, Malawi; Economic Adviser to HM Treasury's External Division, serving with HM Treasury's Delegation, Washington D.C., 1973-74. He was Editor, *Review of the National Institute for Economic and Social Research*, 1976. He was a visiting Hallsworth Research Fellow at Manchester University, 1975 and started the Liverpool Research Group in Macroeconomics in 1979. Professor Minford has been a member of the Monopolies and Mergers Commission since March 1990.

His books include: *Substitution Effects, Speculation and Exchange Rate Stability; Unemployment: Cause and Cure; The Housing Morass;* and a textbook on *Rational Expectations*, with David Peel. He has published various other works on trade, monetary economics and UK and international economy. He has contributed actively to the macroeconomic policy debate in the UK, including a regular column in *The Daily Telegraph*.

Raymond Plant was born 1945. He has been Professor of Politics at the University of Southampton since 1979, and Dean of the Faculty of Social Science from 1981-84. Previously he was a Senior Lecturer in Philosophy at the University of Manchester. His visiting appointments include: Stanton Lecturer, University of Cambridge, 1990 and 1991 and Sarum Lecturer, University of Oxford, 1991. Professor Plant is Chairman of the Labour Party Working Party on Electoral Systems.

He is the author of: *Hegel; Community and Ideology; Political Philosophy and Social Welfare*, with P. Taylor Gooby and H. Lesser; *Philosophy, Politics and Citizenship*, with A. Vincent; *Conservative Capitalism in Britain and the USA: A Critical Appraisal*, with K. Hoover; *Modern Political Thought*; and two Fabian pamphlets, *Equality, Markets and the State*, and *Citizenship, Rights and Socialism*.

Acknowledgements

The thoughts expressed in this paper have been stirred by over a decade of conversation with people of very different viewpoints. Raymond Plant, from a socialist perspective, and Norman Barry, from the perspective of a classical liberal, have been particularly helpful in clarifying my thoughts on the issues addressed in the paper. Conversations over many years with Isaiah Berlin, Samuel Brittan and Joseph Raz have fortified my liberal disposition. Discussions with James Buchanan have helped me formulate better my views on several areas of policy. None of these will necessarily endorse, or accept, the position outlined herein. Nor will most of the other persons whose conversation and comments have over the years been valuable to me—such as Digby Anderson, Donald Hay, Nevil Johnson, Julian Le Grand, Charles King, Eric Mack, David Miller, Michael Noble, Geoffrey Smith, Simon Upton, David Willetts and Andrew Williams. For it is the underlying theme of my argument, entertained by few contemporary thinkers, but argued demonstratively in Joseph Raz's *The Morality of Freedom*, that both egalitarian and libertarian doctrines are fatally flawed and are incapable of serving as fundamental political moralities.

This paper was written during a period as Visiting Distinguished Professor at the Murphy Institute of Political Economy in Tulane. I am indebted to Beanie Kelleher and Ruth Carter for deciphering my longhand and turning it into an elegant typescript, and to Richard Teichgraeber and the other members of the Institute for providing a convivial intellectual environment and an excellent opportunity for research. The paper was completed during a period of residence as Stranahan Distinguished Research Fellow at the Social Philosophy and Policy Center, Bowling Green, Ohio. I am indebted to the Directors and staff of the Center for their valuable support and assistance. I am grateful to David Green for suggesting that a monograph on these issues might be worth writing, and to the IEA Health and Welfare Unit for publishing a paper that is in important respects strongly critical of the standard positions in neo-liberal thought.

John Gray

Introduction

The argument of this paper goes against the current of much recent political thought and practice. It is that both libertarian and egalitarian doctrines are fatally flawed and are therefore incapable of serving as fundamental political moralities. The utopian models suggested by these doctrines—*laissez faire* capitalism and egalitarian socialism—are not only impractical but also, and more importantly, philosophically indefensible. The position here advocated instead is one that has as its central notions satiable basic needs, including that in autonomy, and the rich diversity of options provided by a good community. It is not, as its critics will undoubtedly claim, a muddled pragmatism of the middle ground: it is the only principled position. It has the radical implication that supposedly principled views, such as libertarianism and egalitarianism, are in fact highly indeterminate and barely coherent. It implies, also, for reasons that will be explained, that distributional principles can never be fundamentally important, that the object of policy cannot be the utilitarian one of maximizing collective or aggregate welfare, that political morality can never be based on rights, and that enablement or empowerment of those whose basic needs are not being met has its justification in the necessary conditions of a community rich in inherently public goods rather than in the supposed demands of justice.

The view presented here is that of a liberal market economy constrained (or supplemented) by an enabling welfare state—in other words, a social market economy, as understood in the Freiburg School of Eucken and Erhard, freely applied by the author to the current situation in Britain. This is a view that I would hope could be found worthy of consideration both by liberal conservatives and by liberal-minded social democrats. I spell out the policy implications of this view in the British context primarily, but it doubtless has implications for policy in other countries by way of applications there of the philosophical perspective defended herein, which it is for others to develop, if they wish.

This is a view which seeks to ground the ethical standing of market institutions in their contribution to one of the vital ingredients of individual well-being in the modern world, namely, autonomy. It differs from any classical liberal defence of the market in valuing negative liberty, or freedom from coercion, not in itself, but as an element in autonomy. It further diverges from classical liberalism in holding that the very value that chiefly legitimates market institutions' autonomy, also mandates an enabling welfare state. The classical liberal minimum state is accordingly rejected even as an ideal. The conception of government animating this view is nevertheless that of limited government, inasmuch as the welfare proposals considered devolve as many activities on the institutions of civil society as can be appropriately discharged there and in respect of government are intended to conform to the principle of subsidiarity, with functions being devolved to the lowest feasible and desirable level of government.

The argument developed here diverges from the standard position of contemporary classical liberals in that it is avowedly an ethical argument and not an amoral appeal to the prosperity that market institutions deliver. This reflects the author's conviction that market institutions work well only where their practitioners accord them moral legitimacy—a point relevant especially in the emergent post-communist societies, where the ethical properties of market institutions are little understood and where an amoral defence of the market advocated by many contemporary liberal and libertarian economists only reinforces popular suspicion of it.

It diverges from much standard argumentation on behalf of market institutions, then, in resting its case, not on the contribution made to general or collective welfare by markets, nor on their embodying any imagined system of rights (such as rights to negative liberty), but on their contribution to individual well-being via their enabling individuals to live autonomously in a form of life containing valuable options furnished by a common stock of inherently public goods. The central conception of this account of the ethical foundation of market institutions—of a *satiable basic need*, of the value of *autonomy* and its precondition in a common culture containing a diversity of *inherently public goods*, together with the critique of egalitarianism and libertarianism—are all applications of arguments set out in Joseph Raz's *The Morality of Freedom*, a seminal book which is at once the most important study in liberal philosophy since J.S. Mill's *On Liberty* and the most powerful critique of the currently dominant schools of Anglo-American liberalism. Responsibility for these uses of Raz's arguments remains mine.

A feature of market institutions as enabling devices for individual autonomy that is not mentioned by Raz is their role in enabling agents to act autonomously on their own personal knowledge—knowledge that is typically tacit and practical in form. It is to this epistemic argument for market institutions, often neglected in economic literature and having serious implications for many distributionist and interventionist schemes, that we first turn.

The Epistemic Argument for the Market

What explains the chaos, waste and poverty revealed by the Soviet *glasnost*? What accounts for the ruinous failure of socialist central planning, everywhere in the world? The commonest explanation advanced in Western scholarship involves the perversity of the structure of incentives under which socialist planners, managers and workers must live.[1] There is, no doubt, much force in this explanation. As the Virginia School of Public Choice[2] has taught us, the behaviour of bureaucrats and politicians can be theorized, to a considerable extent, in terms of the economic models used to explain human behaviour in market transactions. The incentive structure created by the Soviet system makes planners risk-averse, inclined to conceal mal-investments by pouring in good money after bad, and disinclined to pursue innovative strategies for which, if they fail, they may be disciplined. Equally, the Soviet manager has an incentive to comply with the quantitative production targets he has been set, regardless of the quality of his products, and to fabricate statistics regarding output. The upshot of this perverse incentive structure can only be a largely chaotic economy, efficient mainly in its parallel sectors, which when it is successful (as it is in some sectors of military technology) is so only at massive and unnecessary cost. In the provision of items necessary for everyday life, the Soviet system cannot avoid being chronically inefficient, since it provides no linkage between consumer preferences and productive effort. Ignorance of these rudimentary truths has led generations of the Western Sovietological *nomenklatura* systematically to overrate performance and productivity in Soviet-type economic systems, with the real situation emerging only in the wake of the Soviet *glasnost* and German reunification. It is only now that it is understood in the West that the low productivity of ordinary workers in the Soviet bloc is to be accounted for by the absence of incentives to work, antiquated plants, the diversion of energy and enterprise into the parallel economy and the endemic wastefulness of logistical and supply systems.

There can, then, be no doubt that the catastrophic failure of Soviet-style planning is in large part to be accounted for by the absence of the benign incentives provided by the disciplines of market competition and the presence of incentives to mismanagement and mal-investment. The deeper explanation of the failure of socialist central planning is, however, not one that appeals to artificial distortion of incentives, but one that invokes instead insuperable limitations of human knowledge. At its simplest, this is expressed in the 'calculation argument', stated classically by L. von Mises, and developed and enriched by Hayek.[3] The Misesian insight is that in any modern economy there will be billions of market exchanges and therefore billions of prices. In the production of any consumer good, for example, producers will need the guidance provided by the prices of many capital goods and these prices will typically be subject to constant change. Because resources and preferences are not static, the structure of relative prices will itself be in a state of constant change. Mises's argument is that, without market pricing of assets, their relative scarcities are unknowable, since simulating market pricing is a calculational impossibility in an economy where billions of market exchanges take place and pricing is in a state of dynamic flux. The limitation of human knowledge identified by Mises's argument is then a calculational limitation. For Mises there cannot be a socialist economy, since rational economic planning by individuals and enterprises is feasible only with the assistance of the information provided by market pricing. One might even say that, for Mises, a socialist system is not an economy at all, but an *anti-economy*.

It was the achievement of Hayek to deepen the Misesian argument and to show that the epistemological difficulty of central planning was far more than calculational. For Hayek, the market is not, primarily, an institution that allocates scarce resources to competing ends. He is concerned to show us that neither the resources available in the economy, nor the variety of uses to which they might be put, is known to anyone. The role of the market is to economize on the scarcest resource of all—human knowledge. The market is for Hayek *an epistemic device*, a discovery procedure for transmitting and indeed generating information that is dispersed throughout society. The epistemic impossibility of successful comprehensive central planning is not for Hayek, as it was for Mises, chiefly a calculational one; it is rather one that flows from the very nature of the knowledge possessed by economic agents. This knowledge, Hayek insists, is not only or mainly the propositional knowledge of basic facts that can easily be theorized or quantified; it is local knowledge of fleeting economic environments, often embodied in skills or practices or expressed in entrepreneurial insight. This is knowledge that by its very nature cannot be collected by a central planning board. Worse, it is knowledge that is squandered if in the attempt to gather it centrally market pricing is suppressed or distorted. The epistemic role of the market, accordingly, is to generate and to make available for general use information (transmitted via price signals) that is irretrievably scattered and cannot be subject to centralisation. The information embodied in market pricing, since it is not the property of any one market participant, is a sort of holistic knowledge of the whole society, a public patrimony that it is the fate of central planning to fritter away. It is this depletion of the stock of knowledge embodied in markets that explains the universal impoverishment of socialist systems.

The deepest and subtlest explanations of the epistemic failure of command economies come not from the Austrian calculation argument of Mises or from its refinement as an argument about the character of knowledge in Hayek. The great achievement of these Austrian arguments was to show that market-simulating planning institutions (such as those proposed in the Lange-Lerner model) were unworkable in any realistically imaginable world because of the impossible demands they made on the knowledge of the planners. It is in the theorizing of Michael Polanyi,[4] in the Polanyian work of Paul Craig Roberts,[5] and in the thought of G.L.S. Shackle,[6] however, that the epistemic impossibilities of successful central planning are given their profoundest statement. Polanyi's argument against central planning of the economy is an application of his argument against the planning of science. In science, progress occurs by diverse scientists and laboratories pursuing divergent lines of inquiry, whose development is not laid down in advance. Each research programme, crucially, is developed in part by the application of that part of the scientist's existing knowledge that is not theorized, and may not be theorizable—the tacit knowledge which he possesses of the practice of science. Polanyi's argument against central planning of science is that, if it could be instituted, it would restrict the resources of further scientific advance to that which is contained in existing theories. It would thereby deny science the indispensable component of tacit knowledge, and so impoverish it. The central planning of science would, for these reasons, retard, or even perhaps reverse, the growth of scientific knowledge.

Polanyi puts to work in his critique of central economic planning the conception of tacit knowledge deployed in his attack on the central planning of scientific research. Tacit knowledge is that vast fund of practical, local and traditional knowledge, embodied in dispositions and forms of life, and expressed in flair and intuition, that can never be formulated in rules of scientific method, for example, and of which our theoretical or articulated knowledge is only the visible tip. In Polanyi's account of it, the most important role of the market is that of a device for the transmission and utilisation of unarticulated, and sometimes inarticulable, tacit and local knowledge. Attempts to collate and collect the tacit knowledge of millions of entrepreneurs and investors are bound to fail, if only because none of them can successfully articulate much of the tacit knowledge he possesses. For this reason, computer simulation of market processes can never be very successful: market participants will always fail to program in that part of their tacit knowledge that is inarticulable. This is to say that such knowledge exists only in use,[7] and is destroyed or depleted when given an articulation that is necessarily partial, abstract, incomplete and defective. The nub of Polanyi's argument against central economic planning is that it is an impossibility because human beings, when they act in markets as in all other areas of conduct, are always ignorant of much of what they know, and so always know more than they can ever say.

The other, deeper reason for the impossibility of successful central economic planning is found in the thought of G.L.S. Shackle, and concerns the unknowability of the future and the subjectivity of expectations. If we have no formula, no algorithm, whereby we can predict or assess the likelihood of future events in the real world, if (in other words) there are singularities and novelties which defeat our inferences from past to future, then a central planning board will merely be wagering when it tries to assess likely future resources and prices. This is, in part, because economies are not self-contained systems, insulated from the rest of human life, in respect of which predictions may be made by way of formal models: they are parts of human life, only separable from the rest in abstraction, and constantly subject to the unpredictable changes wrought by political upheaval, war, fashion and innumerable other causes. Even in the context of the market economy narrowly conceived, we have a kaleidic world that changes, suddenly, and unpredictably, along with changes in subjective expectations. It is a characteristic feature of formal economic models that they suppress the openness of markets to exogenous factors and pass over the unknowability of the future. Economic rationalism has been devastatingly criticised by Shackle, when he writes:[8]

Rationalism, the belief that conduct can be understood as part of the determinate order and process of Nature, into which it is assimilated by virtue of the fact that men choose what is best for them in their circumstances, and their circumstances are laid down by Nature, is a paradox. For it claims to confer upon men freedom to choose, yet to be able to predict what they will choose. It speaks of *choice*, and what can this mean, except that a man is confronted with *rival available* actions? All the actions are available, but all except one are forbidden: forbidden by reasoning self-interest. By assuming that men pursue their desires by applying reason to their circumstances, the analyst can tell what their conduct will be, provided he can also assume that not only he, but they, are in possession of full knowledge of those circumstances? There are the actions of other men, freely chosen by them and constituting part of our individual's circumstances. How can men know each other's concurrent free choices? By pre-reconciliation in a general equilibrium. There is also the future. For the sake of pre-reconciliation of choices, and also for its own unfathomable possibilities, the future must be assumed away. Thus the value-construct describes free, pre-reconciled, determinate choices in a timeless system. It is an arresting triumph of the formal imagination. Beauty, clarity and unity are achieved by a set of axioms as economical as those of classical physical dynamics. Can the real flux of history, personal and public, be approximately understood in terms of this conception? The contrast is such that we have difficulty in achieving any mental collation of the two ideas. Macbeth's despair expresses more nearly the impact of the torrent of events.

Shackle goes on:[9]

The dissolution of belief in the value-theory account of economic affairs was an aspect of the dissolution of Victorian social and international stability. The depressions and business crises of Victorian times could be seen as occasional failures or aberrations of a basically orderly system. British troubles of the 1920s, and world troubles of the 1930s, made this difficult. But they did not overthrow in any lasting way the economists' vested interest in an analyzable economic world. The trouble is that the world is not economic. It is political-economic, it is economic only subject to unappeasable greeds and rivalries and implacable enmities. A general *economic* explanation of economic affairs is an ambition which flies in the face of history and the observable contemporary scene. The economists' only hopeful objective is to provide an account of that shawl of loosely interknotted strands which waves in the wind of the other human influences, political contention, technological invention, explosion of population. He can seek to describe its modes of potential response to each fresh kaleidic shift of the environment, during the time till that shift is superseded by another. But he cannot tell what these shifts will be. Economic affairs are not self-contained or insulated, they cannot have a self-sufficient explanation.

Shackle's argument has been restated by James Buchanan in the context of an appraisal of the work of one of Shackle's most prominent followers, Jack Wiseman:[10]

Mises and Hayek had concentrated on the limits to the availability of knowledge to the central planning agency, by contrast with the knowledge that can be utilized by separate and independent market participants in their localized circumstances. Jack

Wiseman's criticism went well beyond that of Mises and Hayek, and for the first time, demonstrated that the problem was not one of dispersed knowledge *that did indeed exist*. The problem was the wholly different one imposed by the necessity that all choices be made in *time*, and, hence, under conditions of necessary uncertainty. If the future is unknowable, how can decision-makers, whether they be participants in a market or agents acting for the collectivity, be made accountable? How can any monitor check on the competence and the integrity of the chooser, other than through the observation of results? How, then, can we lay down a rule to be followed, in advance of the conditions to be encountered? Where is the collectivist equivalent of the bankruptcy court?

In Buchanan's restatement of it, the Shacklean argument against central economic planning invokes the *non-existence* of the knowledge which planners would need were they to be able to plan successfully. Like actors in a market, central planners are forever denied knowledge of the future. By comparison with market participants, however, planners will make larger errors—errors for which there is no elimination device such as bankruptcy in markets. Markets may, indeed, exhibit speculative manias and panics, as subjective expectations ebb and flow; they are not spared the fate of perpetual ignorance or un-knowledge (in Shackle's neologism) which is an inexorable consequence of our nature as time-bound creatures for whom the future can only be guesswork.[11] We are on safer ground, however, if in an irredeemably uncertain world we trust to the diverse expectations and plans of many market participants rather than the monism of the plan, with its narrow and inevitably arbitrary expectations of the future. Shackle's argument is, in its way, a necessary complement to Polanyi's: we are always, according to Shackle, ignorant of what it is that we do not know, even as (according to Polanyi) we always know more than we can ever say. It is through these Polanyian and Shacklean insights that the epistemic impossibilities of central planning are best explained.

If central economic planning is an impossibility for these deeper epistemic reasons, what do we have in so-called command economies? It is the achievement of Paul Craig Roberts,[12] virtually alone, to have theorized in an illuminating way the realities of economic life under Soviet-style planning institutions. Roberts shows that such economies must in practice invariably be polycentric, with the plan reflecting, rather than dictating, the behaviour of managers, suppliers and workers. Since the planners inevitably lack the knowledge, tacit and articulated, necessary to any successful economic project, local managers must make their own local arrangements (with suppliers, and so forth), relying on their own local knowledge. Accordingly, the formal and the informal, the official and the parallel economies are at every point intimately and inextricably related, with the official economy achieving any degree of success only in virtue of its dependency on the institutions of the parallel economy. Quite apart from the unreliability and fictitious character of Soviet economic statistics, the gigantism of the Five Year Plans, for example, masked the permanent Soviet reality of polycentrism, in which the Plan functions chiefly as a summation, partly fictitious, of the activities of managers, who achieve as much as they do in virtue of their reliance on surviving market prices—in particular, historic, global and black market prices.

It is only in virtue of the immense resourcefulness of the Soviet peoples in devising and using these manifold informal economic institutions—in reinventing the market against the background of political institutions committed (at least until recently) to the suppression of commodity-production—that social and economic life in the Soviet Union has managed to renew itself at all. The failure of *perestroika*, indeed, arises from the fact that it encompasses both a partial dismantlement of the central planning institutions and an attack on the least inefficient part of the economy—its parallel sector.

The epistemic argument for the market, most profoundly developed in the work of Polanyi and Roberts, provides a sound theoretical explanation of the systemic failures of socialist command economies everywhere. It shows why, even putting their rejection of consumer sovereignty on one side, the Soviet elites find achieving their own economic goals, including those relating to the Soviet military industrial complex, extraordinarily costly and difficult. It is indeed probably the case that the initial motivation of *glasnost* was in the realisation that, even in military technology, to which a massive proportion of GNP was being committed, the Soviet Union was in certain respects falling behind the West, and above all could not hope fully to replicate the American Strategic Defence Initiative.[13] Further, the Polanyian and Shacklean arguments demonstrate that, even if the Soviet leadership had been successful in creating a new *homo sovieticus*, which would not respond to the perverse incentive structure created by the planning institutions but would mechanically follow planning objectives, he would lack the knowledge needed to achieve the planners' goals. The Soviet system, or any modelled on it, thus reproduces on a vast scale all the irrationalities prophetically foreseen by Tolstoy, when he criticised plans for a 'rational agriculture' in his novel, *War and Peace*.[14] From this point of view, we can represent socialist central planning as the reverse of the epistemic device of the market—as a device for wasting, depleting and finally destroying the tacit knowledge that is indispensable in economic life.

A number of caveats are worth making at this point. The epistemic argument for market institutions does not mean that, in the absence of a full blown market economy, nothing of economic importance can be achieved. On the contrary, markets can be simulated or replicated, as they were in the Soviet Union when Stalin in 1939 created seventeen competing design bureaux for fighter aircraft, some of which were based in the *sharashka*, the special scientific institutes staffed by *Gulag* prisoners.[15] The sophistication of Soviet military technology, some of it known now to be far in advance of anything possessed in the West, shows that the idea that technological innovation requires economic or personal liberty is merely another liberal illusion.[16] Nor is it being asserted that in the consumer economy from whose chaos the strategic, military economy is largely insulated, nothing can be achieved by the planning institutions. Again, on the contrary when (as in Czechoslovakia in the Sixties) they have confined themselves to producing a few staple commodities, they have achieved a measure of success. What the epistemic argument does tell us is that, in the absence of effective price mechanism that can only be provided by market institutions, there will inevitably be massive waste and mal-investment, with even the strategic military sector achieving what it does at the cost of something between 25 and 50 per cent of GNP being devoted to it (a percentage that has not changed since the events of August 1991). In short, the upshot of the epistemic argument is not that central planning institutions always fail, but that even their successes carry heavy and unnecessary human and economic costs. That socialist institutions everywhere generate poverty is to be explained partly by the epistemic argument, but partly also by the lack of incentives in the consumer economy. Taken together, the epistemic and the incentive arguments enable us to predict that central planning institutions will be wasteful and inefficient wherever they are set up, regardless of the cultural and economic environment in which they find themselves. The poverty of the Russians has, then, nothing to do with the alleged defects of the Slav work ethic: it has the same explanation—in the epistemic and incentive defects of central planning institutions—as the poverty of Cubans, Mongols and Balts.

Though they are distinct, the epistemic argument and the argument from incentives are complementary rather than competitive in their role as theoretical rationales for the market economy. They also have a common core. For the incentive argument invokes the fact that planning institutions obstruct the individual in acting upon his projects and purposes, while the epistemic argument notes that they prevent him from using and benefitting from his own knowledge. In both cases, the planning institutions constrain or diminish the autonomy of the individual, partly by compelling him to act on purposes that are not his own, partly by depriving him of the opportunity to engage in projects animated by his own knowledge. The common feature of both arguments for the market is that they identify the detrimental impact of socialist central planning institutions on individual autonomy. This suggests that the epistemic device of the market has an ethical implication, or presupposition—that the market protects or enhances the autonomy of the individual. It has also a policy implication, to which I shall return when in Chapter Five I develop the case against market socialism. The policy implication of the epistemic argument, in its Austrian as well as its Polanyian and Shacklean forms, is that economic rationality demands not only market pricing of most factors of production, but also (partly as a precondition of genuine market pricing) their private ownership. Why is this? The reason is to be found in the fact that individuals are most likely to be able to deploy their personal tacit knowledge when they are least constrained by collective decision-procedures in which this knowledge is diluted or lost. (This is, perhaps, especially true of that species of tacit knowledge which is expressed in entrepreneurial insight.) In order to be able to make the best of their personal fund of tacit knowledge, individuals need a domain in which they may act solely on their own judgment (and, of course, at their own risk). Such a domain is provided by private property in productive assets. (As I shall later argue, the institution of private or several property in a modern economy is likely to be embodied in the form of the capitalist corporation; but this need not always be so.) The epistemic and the incentive arguments come together in endorsing the institution of private property as a necessary condition of economic rationality. They also legitimate private property as a precondition of individual autonomy.

It may be objected, against the argument just developed, that much of modern business life is conducted via the bureaucratic structures of large corporations, in which individuals have little opportunity to act directly on their own initiative. Against this objection, one might respond that much innovation emerges from the small business sector, which thereby acts as a competitive constraint on the conservative tendencies of the larger firms. This would not, however, be the most fundamentally compelling response. The more powerful rejoinder would be an appeal to the body of theory developed by Alchian, Manne, Winter and Pelikan[17] on the contribution made to dynamic efficiency by the operation of the market for corporate control. In the somewhat evolutionary perspective developed by these writers, the market for corporate control, that is to say, the threat of takeover, acts as a filter device for the economic competence of managers. As Pelikan makes clear,[18] the economic competence of managers has as a crucial component their tacit knowledge of their business environments. The effect of the workings of the market for corporate control, at least to some degree, is selective pressure against less competent management, and the imposition of a competitive constraint on those that survive. Market competition for corporate control in this way replicates to some extent the individual's reliance on personal tacit knowledge by the entrepreneur acting directly on his own initiative.[19] Most fundamentally, however, the objection that modern corporations engage in large-scale, long-term planning neglects the evident fact that such corporations exist within, and are subject to the constraints of, a global competitive market. Bureaucratic planners in such corporations must heed the threat of actual and potential competitors in their strategies. If they do not (*pace* the Chrysler corporation) then they will fail. Unlike socialist planners, then, the planners of a modern corporation cannot (unless they acquire monopolistic governmental privileges) insulate themselves from market competition. It is this crucial distinction between the situations of corporate and socialist planners that defeats the objection to the argument considered above.

The epistemic and the incentive arguments for the market, especially when taken together, are overwhelming. They show us why and how prosperity in a modern economy can be achieved only through the medium of market institutions. These arguments are nevertheless deficient. As they stand, they are morally virtually empty, even if they have some ethical implications and presuppositions. They tell us that only the market can deliver us the goods, but they leave moral criticism of the market economy unanswered. A critic of the market might accept all that has been argued here about the indispensable efficiencies of the market, and yet attack it on ethical grounds. He might argue that unfettered markets promote greed and envy, shatter communities, and debase cultural values. More radically, he might deny that markets promote individual autonomy, and maintain that we are constrained rather than emancipated by participating in markets. He might focus critically on the distributional effects and preconditions of market economies, holding that they necessitate or reproduce structural inequalities in life-chances that are morally unacceptable. And, more simply but no less powerfully, he might draw our attention to the situation of those, lacking in skills or resources, whose plight prevents them from fully participating in the market or enjoying many of its benefits. Such a critic of the market might, in other words, accept all the criticisms that I have made of socialist planning institutions, and yet deny that the market economy has any real ethical standing.[20] As the argument I have developed goes so far, such a critic could claim to occupy the high moral ground, with the defender of the market appearing as a grubby pragmatist, ready and willing to sacrifice important ethical values for the sake of mere material prosperity. It remains to be seen if this, potentially fatal weakness in the case for the market can be remedied.

3

The Illusions of Libertarianism

The upshot of the epistemic argument for the market is that, because he is denied the knowledge of relative scarcities given only by market prices, the socialist manager is bound to fail to achieve the objectives set for him by the central planning board, or to achieve them only at vast and unnecessary cost. This will be so, whatever the objectives and motivations of the planners, and even if they have no other reason for action than obedience to the plan. If the epistemic argument is well-founded, even a population of socialist saints would be impoverished.

Socialist central planning invariably results in mass poverty, precisely because of its adverse impact on human autonomy. It is, in truth, in its indispensable role as one of the chief preconditions of the autonomy of the individual that the ethical standing of the market lies. The free market enables the individual to act upon his own goals and values, his objectives and his plan of life, without subordination to any other individual or subjection to any collective decision procedure. It is from its role as *an enabling device* for the protection and enhancement of human autonomy that the ethical justification of the market is ultimately derived. It is important to distinguish this ethical justification of the market from two other defences, often found in classical liberal and conservative writers. The first is the defence that, under market institutions, economic growth is maximised, and with it the choices available to individuals. This is a weak argument for several reasons. Though the promotion of economic growth may be forced upon modern governments by the pressures of political competition in mass democracies, economic growth, in and of itself, has no ethical standing. Nor is it at all self-evident that economic growth, as such, always enlarges or enhances choice-making.[21] It may or may not make a contribution to that which in the end matters in ethics and politics—human well-being. There is also an aggregative illusion in all the quantitative measures used in macro-economic theorizing. These measures—of GNP or money supply, say—may have limited, pragmatic uses for the purposes of policy, but they always involve a simplification of and an abstraction from the human realities which undermines any claim made on their behalf in ethical terms. The human reality is that of distinct individuals, pursuing disparate and sometimes incommensurable ends, whose satisfactions cannot be weighed or ranked on any single measure. The theory of economic life of the classical economists, in which economics was conceived as a science of plutology, or wealth creation, rests on a communistic fiction in which it is supposed that resources and satisfactions are, in principle at least, knowable and measurable. It is the insight of the Austrian economists, but also, and above all, of Shackle,[22] that, even under the institutions of an unhampered market our aggregative assessments always contain elements of the conventional, the fictitious and the arbitrary. Artificial constructs of this kind cannot be supposed to possess any kind of ethical standing.

This is to state in other terms the classical objection to liberal utilitarianism.[23] In any of its many varieties, utilitarianism presupposes that an interpersonal comparison of utilities is a real possibility. On the view presented here, we can rarely, except in limiting cases, possess the knowledge required for such judgments. And this is not just in virtue of any remediable imperfection in our understanding, it is because of incommensurabilities among the various goods that go to make up human well-being.[24] In many cases, it is not even in principle possible to render the diverse ingredients of the good rationally comparable. For this reason, it is often impossible to make comparative utility assessments even within a single individual's life. It follows that any defense of the market, say, which stresses its role as a maximizer of utility, of desire-satisfaction or whatever, has fallen victim to a fallacy of conceptual realism.

This is, indeed, the ultimate argument against any political morality that claims to be utilitarian—that it has as its fundamental value, or maximand, a figment, general welfare, when the reality is that of distinct individuals pursuing incommensurable values. It is on this fallacy that liberal utilitarianism in all its forms founders. More specifically, the defence of the market is, for this reason, best conducted not in terms of its contribution to an imaginary general or collective welfare, but instead by reference to its role in contributing to the well-being of the individual.

It is at this point that the defense of the market in ethical terms that is developed here diverges in a second way from the standard justification advanced by classical liberals and conservatives. These invariably focus on the role of the market as a shield against political coercion and on its contribution to the dispersal of power in society—in short, on its contribution to negative freedom.[25] This conventional classical liberal position is a dead end for a variety of reasons. Let us at once set aside the sterile activity of linguistic or conceptual analysis, since it is evident that there is no consensus among us as to the meaning of freedom or liberty that could settle substantive questions in ethics and politics. (It may be worth noting, in parenthesis, that nothing important in Berlin's seminal defence of negative liberty turns on such semantic considerations.)[26] What interests us is not the uses in ordinary language of the terms 'liberty' or 'freedom', but instead the reasons why freedom or liberty itself is valuable. Here the weakness of the conventional classical liberal view is manifest. What, if anything, is intrinsically valuable about the negative freedom of absence of coercion?[27] If the answer is that it facilitates the satisfaction of wants, then the position that has then emerged is one that will license abridgement of negative freedom whenever want-satisfaction is thereby increased. This does not seem a very principled line of defence of the free market.

The view that negative freedom is itself an intrinsic value fares no better. What is intrinsically valuable about it? The idea that negative freedom is a value that should be maximized or optimized in any case breaks down on the awkward fact that we have no agreed procedure for measuring or weighing on-balance freedom. Except in limiting cases, we find that judgments about 'the greatest freedom' are invariably controversial, in that they invoke rival conceptions of what is good and choiceworthy. This indeterminacy in the very notion of negative liberty spells ruin for the classical liberal project of stating a principle—Spencer's principle of Greatest Equal Freedom, say, or J. S. Mill's 'one very simple principle' about not restraining liberty save where harm to others is at issue—that can authoritatively guide thought and policy on the restraint of liberty. Because we cannot identify 'the greatest liberty', principles which speak of maximizing it are empty. To talk, as classical liberals still do, of minimizing coercion by maximizing negative liberty, is merely to traffic in illusions. The objection to negative liberty, taken in and of itself, is that its content is radically indeterminate, just as its intrinsic value is negligible. For these reasons, it is highly implausible that any political morality can be defended that has at its foundation a supposed basic right or claim to negative liberty.

The value of negative liberty must therefore be theorized in terms of its contribution to something other than itself, which does possess intrinsic value. In truth, it seems clear that the chief value of negative liberty is in its contribution to the positive liberty of autonomy. By autonomy is meant the condition in which a person can be at least part author of his life, in that he has before him a range of worthwhile options, in respect of which his choices are not fettered by coercion and with regard to which he possesses the capacities and resources presupposed by a reasonable measure of success in his self-chosen path among these options.

It is clear that autonomy is a complex status, not definable by reference to the presence or absence of any single condition. As Raz has put it, with a clarity and conciseness on which I cannot hope to improve:

> It is wrong to identify autonomy with a right against coercion, and to hold that right (i.e., the right against coercion) as defeating, because of the importance of personal autonomy, all, or almost all, other considerations. Many rights contribute to making autonomy possible, but no short list of concrete rights is sufficient for this purpose. The provision of many collective goods is constitutive of the very possibility of autonomy and it cannot be relegated to a subordinate role, compared with some alleged right against coercion, in the name of autonomy.[28]

Raz's insight here is of vital importance. The conditions under which a person enjoys a decent measure of autonomy are many and various, and cannot be covered by the umbrella of a single right. It is patently obvious that autonomy is far more than the mere absence of coercion by others, since it is self-evident that that condition may co-exist with a complete inability to achieve any important objective or purpose. This is a point of some considerable importance, as we shall see when in Chapter Three we consider the case for an enabling welfare state.

The ethical standing of the market is its status as a necessary condition of one vital ingredient of human well-being, individual autonomy. Unlike any political procedure for the allocation of resources, free markets enable individuals to command goods and services on their terms, and to exit from forms of provision that displease them. The freedom of autonomous individuals in markets is not that of *voice* (having a role in collective decision making), but typically that of *exit*.[29] In any collective decision-procedure, as Hayek has observed,[30] individuals will be constrained in their choices by the common or majority opinion of what is desirable, or even possible. By contrast with political institutions that require a policy binding on all, markets allow each to go his own way, thus allowing an exfoliation of individuality and diversity. Markets are by their nature sensitive to differences among people, and hostile to the Procrustean conformism of the central plan.

It may be worth pausing at this stage of the argument to correct some common misconceptions of the moral standing of the market. It is a piece of conventional wisdom about the market that it promotes or depends upon egoism, and therefore discriminates against altruism and sympathy. This common prejudice neglects several important features of market institutions, and of the realistic alternatives to them. It is often associated with the primitive misconception that human behaviour in collective or political institutions is less likely to be egoistic than altruistic—a belief for which there is no evidence whatever. Both common sense observation, and the theorizings of the Virginia Public Choice School, suggest that human beings in political contexts are animated by the same motives that dominate market exchanges. There is this difference, however, whereas market exchanges are voluntaristic transactions which typically benefit all parties to them, political transactions are often zero-sum, or even negative-sum exchanges in which what is gained by one is lost by another. This Smithian insight about the mutual advantageousness of voluntary exchange leads to another—that the motives which animate market exchange are mixed, and need not be (and usually are not) purely egoistic. When a businessman seeks to make a profit, his motive may be to enrich himself or his family; but it may also be to endow a university chair. When a consumer seeks the lowest price for a product, his motive may be to economise on expense so as to build up his own fortune; but the consumer may be acting on behalf of a charitable organization, and may be seeking the lowest prices so as to better promote its good works. There is, in truth, no uniformity, but rather considerable diversity, in the motives that animate people as they enter into market exchanges.

The prejudice that markets promote egoism, while collective procedures facilitate altruism, is, if anything, the reverse of the truth. As anyone familiar with life in Soviet lands knows all too well, the reality of everyday existence there is one of incessant mutual predation and necessitous bargaining. The caricature of *laissez-faire* capitalism in which all relationships are turned into market exchanges applies far better to the socialist societies than to any market economy. The reason for this is that, in socialist societies, many goods—such as housing or education, and now perhaps even food—that in market economies are generally available to all, are there *positional goods*, acquired through the Party or its subsidiary networks. The competition for positional goods is, by its very nature, a zero-sum conflict, since a positional good is one that cannot be possessed or consumed by all. In socialist systems, access even to the goods essential to daily living depends to a considerable extent on possession of the supreme and paradigm positional good—that of power. It is a virtue of the market economy that in it access to most goods depends solely on ability and willingness to pay for them.

Conventional academic wisdom about the market has also gone astray in neglecting the virtues that market systems inculcate or demand in people. These encompass not only honesty and diligence, but also sensitivity to the needs and preferences of others. In predatory Soviet-style systems, the virtues that are at a premium are the Hobbesian ones, appropriate to his hypothetical state of nature, of force and fraud, coercion and deception. By contrast, the virtues elicited in market economies are those of the autonomous person—the person (in Feinberg's excellent account)[31] who is self-possessed, who has a distinct self-identity or individuality, who is authentic and self-directed, and whose life is to some significant degree a matter of self-creation. These autonomy-dependent virtues may not be characteristic of *all* market systems, since East Asian Confucian-inspired market orders may function perfectly well without many of them, but they animate all of the market systems whose inheritance is, like ours, an individualist moral culture.

Market systems of our kind, then, depend upon and reward autonomy-based virtues. They are far from being amoral instruments of wealth-creation. Nor is the autonomy they foster the bohemian, antinomian or nihilistic autonomy which some have found in J.S. Mill's *On Liberty*, and which has been devastatingly criticised by Lomasky.[32] The autonomy to which I refer here may exist to some extent, and indeed flourish, even in cultures (such as those of East Asia) which are not individualist in their moral inheritance. There, as among us, market exchange occurs among persons responsible for their choices in voluntary transactions. In these cultures, voluntaristic human agency is pervasive, even if western ideals of autonomy are not prized, and it is arguable that, in a broader sense of autonomy in which it encompasses the ascription to persons of responsibility, autonomy animates even those market systems which are not based on individualism. Indeed, even in a culture from which autonomy was absent, if such be conceivable, the market economy would remain as an expression of voluntary human agency without which no modern society can successfully reproduce itself. The autonomy fostered by market orders is, then, that of independence and responsibility, not that of the free-floating sovereign self, or the rootless author of the *acte gratuite*.

Autonomy-based market systems are therefore fully compatible with tradition and community, since autonomous men and women will typically emerge from strong and stable communities and will remain embedded in them. In general, the twentieth century decimation and destruction of communities has been the work, principally, not of markets but of governments, from the genocidal terror of the Chinese communist government in Tibet to the desolation wreaked on working class communities in Britain by municipal projects of urban renewal. All the evidence suggests that, left to their own devices, people will in free markets renew their traditions and communities rather than desert or destroy them. For in promoting autonomy and enabling its exercise, the market also, and necessarily, promotes and rewards virtues of a sort required by a voluntarist culture.

In invoking their role as enabling devices for human autonomy to explain the ethical standing of markets, it is important to be clear as to what is not here being claimed. It is *not* claimed that autonomy is an essential ingredient in any good life, nor even that the best human life will of necessity be an autonomous one. Perhaps, when comparing autonomous with non-autonomous forms of life, non-autonomous ones may emerge sometimes as superior forms of human flourishing. (Compare the forms of life of medieval Christendom, or of Japan in the Edo period, with those of the contemporary American inner city.) Or perhaps we are here in a realm of incommensurables. At any rate, the claim being made here is not that autonomy is a universal good, but that it is an essential element in any good life that can be lived *by us*. No inhabitant of a modern pluralistic, mobile and discursive society can fare well without at least a modicum of the capacities and resources needed for autonomy.[33] Most modern societies are such, in other words, that the constitutive ingredients of autonomy—the capacity for rational deliberation and choice, the absence of coercion by others and the possession of the resources needed for a life that is at least partly self-directed—are among our most vital interests. They are, indeed, vital ingredients in our well-being as a whole.

Autonomy is not then a necessary element in human flourishing *tout court*. It is an essential element of the good life for people situated in our historical context as inheritors of a particular, individualist form of life. The conditions constitutive of, and demanded by autonomy are therefore not universal human rights, but conditions that are to a considerable degree culture-specific. Nor are they the same for all members even of our own culture. As Raz has observed in the passage already quoted, there is an essential indeterminacy in any account of the rights that support autonomy, since no complete or exhaustive list of them can be made. Nevertheless, we can clearly see that the conditions necessary for the autonomy of a disabled person, say, may well require the possession and exercise of claims which the able-bodied may not legitimately have. To say this is only to make the commonsense point that circumstances alter cases, and the conditions of autonomy may vary across persons, or, for that matter, may alter over time, during a single person's life. The content of the conditions that contribute to the autonomy of a person with Alzheimer's Disease may well differ from those that contribute to his autonomy before the illness struck him, since the kinds and degree of autonomy achievable by him may well now have altered, and the place of autonomy in the interests vital to his well-being may also have changed.

The conditions that enter into and support individual autonomy will be subject to considerable variation. Even among the modernist societies in which autonomy is a vital ingredient in human well-being, there are divergent conditions and inheritances, different resource levels and forms of political and moral culture and of economic and social life, which mean that the detailed pattern of rights promoting autonomy will vary significantly. The content of the conditions promoting autonomy has then an ineliminable dimension that is cultural and conventional. But, within these broader variations, the content of autonomy rights (as we may term them) will also vary according to the categories of the persons concerned—their abilities or disabilities, their position in the human life cycle, their resources, their needs, and so on. With respect to autonomy, it is not remotely plausible to suppose that its conditions can be specified in any fixed and highly determinate set of basic entitlements or liberties. To suppose that this is possible is to fall prey to the legalist illusion that animates much recent theorizing, especially that of Rawls,[34] and which is a perpetual temptation for liberal thought.[35]

It is because the classical liberal idea that our liberties, negative and positive, can be specified, once and for all, in a highly determinate fashion, is a mere illusion that I shall reject the idea that the conditions which support and ground autonomy can or should be theorized as rights. While criticising the standard neo-liberal arguments against positive or welfare rights, I shall maintain that the preconditions of autonomy are too complex, too variable and too diverse to be captured in the legalist discourse of rights. They encompass, among other things, a broad diversity of institutions aiming to provide the conditions of autonomous action, as well as a rich and deep common culture containing choice-worthy options and forms of life. In theorizing autonomy as the primary animating value of market institutions and of a liberal civil society, we should (as I shall argue) resist the rigidity of the legalist discourse of rights; and instead acknowledge the dependency of autonomous thought and actions on a whole range of institutions, conventions and forms of life whose structure and content eludes purblind perspectives of rights theory.

Three final caveats may be worth mentioning. It is not being argued that the institutions of the market have any unique role in promoting and enhancing individual autonomy. That value is also promoted in voluntary associations—families, churches and many other forms of life—in which market exchange is peripheral. The claim is not that market institutions alone promote autonomy in society, but rather that in their absence people will be denied autonomy in a vital part of their lives—the economic dimension in which they act as consumers and producers. Indeed, far more is needed for reasonably autonomous persons than the market economy—in particular, as I shall argue, a system of welfare institutions which guarantees the resource conditions of autonomy to all, and a rich public culture and forms of common life which offers people a wide array of worthwhile options.

Nor is it at any point in the argument assumed that the institutions of the market are given to us once and for all, or that they will be everywhere the same. On the view presented here—a view inspired by the social market theory of the Freiburg School—the market is not a natural datum, but (like every other human institution) an artifact—and an extremely complex artifact at that. We must not suppose, as the delusive perspectives of *laissez-faire* philosophy encourage us to do, that the free market is what remains after all control and regulation has been abolished. The forms of property, and of contractual liberty, which go to make up the market are themselves legal artifacts, human constructs that human design may amend or reform. The idea, common among latter-day classical liberals, of the market as a spontaneous order, may be illuminating insofar as it generates insight into the ways in which unplanned market exchanges may coordinate human activities better than any plan; but it is profoundly misleading if it suggests that the institutional framework of the market process is given to us as a natural fact, or can be deduced from any simple theory. There will, in fact, be considerable variation, across countries and over time, in the forms of property, the varieties and limits of contractual liberty and the kinds of competition which the institutions of the market encompass. The view of the market that is to be rejected, accordingly, is that which theorizes its institutions as flowing from some underlying structure of rights. On the contrary view developed here, market institutions, like rights themselves, are social artifacts whose justification is in their contribution to human well-being. If, as I have argued, markets are to be justified in that fashion, and, in particular, by reference to their contribution to autonomy, then it follows that they may also be reformed or redesigned, when their contribution to that interest is compromised. That this is no merely formal or abstract point will be seen in the last chapter of this paper, when I consider how government policy may complement and inform the market process.

Thirdly, and finally, it is not here claimed that it is in their contribution to autonomy that the sole or exclusive justification of market institutions is to be found. Such a claim would be wholly contrary to the Berlinian value-pluralism that animates the argument here advanced. Rather, the argument is that it is the contribution made to autonomy by market institutions that gives them their deepest, and most neglected justification for us. Doubtless market institutions promote many other good things: but it is their role as enabling devices for autonomy that is focused upon here, partly in response to the inadequacies of the standard liberal defence of them in terms of their contribution to negative liberty. The argument is, then, that it is in their contribution to autonomous thought and action that the primary value of market institutions lies for us.

It is evident that the defence of the market as an enabling institution for individual autonomy has important implications for the matrix of claims which people possess when they enter the market economy. If, as I have argued, the morally unsatisfactory idea of negative freedom cannot account for the ethical standing of the market, then it is plausible to suppose that the entitlements or claims which people possess as they enter the market cannot coherently be restricted to those which grant them immunity from coercion by others. They will also be positive claims that guarantee a decent array of worthwhile options and which confer upon people entitlements to resources. At this point, a crucial feature of the logic of the ethical defense of the market becomes apparent. This is that the argument which justifies free markets as enabling devices for autonomous choices also, and inexorably, justifies the institution of an enabling welfare state, where this is among the conditions of autonomous choice and action. Before we set out the purposes and policies of such a state, however, it is worth examining why two common alternatives to the social market model advanced here, egalitarianism and market socialism—are indefensible and should be removed from the intellectual and political agenda.

4

The Mirage of
Egalitarianism

The enabling welfare state to be advocated in Chapter Six of this
paper is meant to guarantee far more than the subsistence
claims acknowledged in classical liberal thought. The welfare
claims defended in the argument go well beyond subsistence
claims, since they are claims to the satisfaction of basic needs,
including that in autonomy. In defending and advocating such
an enabling welfare state, I have rejected as rationally
indefensible and morally superficial the libertarian view that the
scope of a limited government is confined to the sphere of
passive rights to negative liberty.

In rejecting this conventional libertarian position, am I not
occupying an unstable middle ground between libertarian and
egalitarian positions? In particular, why do I stop short of
accepting equality of well-being, say, or of the value of autonomy, as a legitimate goal of policy? It is the burden of Raymond
Plant's argument[36] that a commitment to egalitarianism is
necessitated by any liberal position which aims, as mine does,
to empower or enable people in the satisfaction of their basic
needs. Plant's argument seems to have two prongs, one normative, the other empirical. The normative one is the appeal to a
principle requiring that people's well-being, or the value of their
liberty, be equalised. The empirical argument is the thesis that,
if the goal is the empowerment of the needy and if power is a
positional good, then guaranteeing basic need-satisfaction will
often generate zero-sum exchanges in which a rule of equality
would seem to be the only fair distributional principle.

Neither of these arguments shows the rationality of egalitarianism, or addresses its most serious difficulties. The normative
principle neglects the satiability of most basic needs, including

those connected with autonomy and has the flaws (later to be explored) of all distributional principles that are designed to have a foundational role in a political morality. If most basic needs are indeed satiable, as I have argued, then the welfare claims they generate can be met completely, and without remainder. More specifically, Plant's argument is defective in that it follows the early Rawls in conceiving liberty as a variable that can indefinitely be maximized. On the account of autonomy given here, this is a mistake. Autonomy is best theorized as a basic need that is satiable. Though the level at which its satiation occurs may vary across and even within societies, there is nothing in the nature of things which prevents us from specifying the conditions under which the basic need of autonomy has been satisfied. Consider again the instructive example of the severely disabled person. If, let us say, we consider two people with the same, severe disability, where one is a millionaire and lives in the Ritz Hotel, and the other lacks resources and is provided for by disability benefits, but where *both* persons enjoy the conditions necessary for a dignified, meaningful and autonomous life, then in my view the difference in the level of resource-provision of the two disabled persons has no moral significance. If both have good lives, why should the difference between them in terms of wealth concern us at all?

The answer given by Plant—an answer which invokes some principle regarding the equalisation of human well-being or the value of liberty—begs the question and has deep difficulties. It is not shown *why* justice demands equality in any of its forms. The suggestion is counter-intuitive, given that it neglects considerations of desert as well as of need. Again, no principle of equality is stated by Plant, save perhaps the principle demanding equal value of liberty. It is unclear that this is a workable principle, given the difficulties associated with the making of interpersonal utility comparisons: if there are incommensurabilities as between the goods of different persons, then these incommensurabilities will be just as much an impediment to an egalitarian deontic morality as they are to a consequentialist ethic. (If there are incommensurabilities among liberties and among the values they possess for their holders, how can we ever know when the value of liberty has been equalised? Is it supposed that we can construct a libertarian calculus?) Alternative egalitarian principles that do not demand or depend upon such utility assessment fare no better. The demand for equalisation of resources, if it could be given any definite content, would prove counter-intuitive because it fails to give weight to handicap.

Rawls's famous Difference, or Maximin Principle, which affirms that only that degree of inequality is just which elevates the position of the worst-off to the highest level possible, is indeterminate as to the degree of inequality it sanctions and makes impossible demands on the knowledge of policy-makers. (Again, how could anyone ever *know* when the level of the worst-off had been maximised?) And Dworkin's principle of equal concern and respect is hopelessly indeterminate, its content being given by the ephemera of American academic conventional wisdom rather than by any form of principled reasoning.

The empirical side of Plant's argument depends on claims about the operation of markets that are highly controversial and on a view of empowerment that is misconceived. Market exchanges are very rarely zero-sum transactions in which what one gains the other loses. Indeed, it is precisely the character of market exchange as a transaction that is typically positive-sum, and so advantageous to both parties, that distinguishes it from most forms of political resource allocation. Plant has provided us with no empirical evidence that shows, or even suggests, that market provision of services typically renders them positional goods.

It seems, in fact, that Plant's argument rests on a conceptual fallacy rather than upon theory or evidence. It is true that political power is a positional good, and can be nothing else. It is for this reason that, in societies where resource allocation is highly politicised, goods that are not positional in market economies often become markedly so. In the communist regimes, for example, goods such as housing, medical care, education and even food, that in the West are not significantly positional, become positional because access to them is mediated by the institutions of the Party and its corrupt and exploitative *nomenklatura*. In other words, the allocation of goods via political power is bound to enhance their positionality, or to render them positional when they were not so before, in virtue of the fact that access to the political power of the Party cannot in its nature be equally distributed. For this reason, the positionality of the good of political power tells against the political allocation of resources and speaks in favour of their allocation by markets.

The conceptual fallacy in Plant's argument is in assimilating the empowerment of the poor and the needy to the model of political power. Empowerment, or better, enablement, as I understand it, means conferring on such people the opportunities and the resources they need to live autonomously. It is thoroughly unclear, and Plant gives us no reason to suppose, that the enablement of any one person necessarily, or even commonly, entails the disablement of any other. How do welfare benefits for the disabled, perhaps framed in terms of voucher schemes, limit or disempower the able-bodied? In general, such schemes will have the effect of enhancing autonomy in the population, without incurring any cost in the heteronomy of others. Because it is a satiable good, autonomy—the basis of many of the welfare benefits that are defended here—is rarely, if ever a positional good. Plant's argument seems to invoke, not any scarcity or conflict in the real world, but instead a conceptual claim that has no leverage on policies that aim to empower or enable people to act autonomously in markets. It leaves unanswered the crucial question: if, in the real world, positional goods are rarer and less important for individual well-being than Plant supposes, what does that portend for Plant's commitment to equality? Would it (in other words) make sense to be an egalitarian in a world (if such there could be) without positional goods? It is the confusion of empirical and conceptual claims that prevents Plant's argument from addressing these hard questions.

Plant's egalitarianism depends crucially on this conceptual error, and its conflated empirical claims, and has few arguments at its disposal without it. It remains to look at the flaws, and indeed the incoherencies, of all forms of egalitarianism, flaws that are not unique to egalitarianism, but which affect any political morality that is supposed to be distributionist at its foundation. Let us consider the flaws, first, of egalitarianism. It has many implications (whatever specific egalitarian principle is under consideration) that are absurd or offensive. As Raz has noted,[37] egalitarian principles are indifferent between achieving equality through taking away from those who have and giving to those who have not. Further, the only intrinsic goods and evils egalitarian principles recognise are relational ones. As Raz observes, decisively:[38]

> If they (egalitarian principles) constitute the entire foundation of morality then the happiness of a person does not matter except if there are other happy people. Nor is there any reason to avoid harming or hurting a person except on the ground that there are others who are unharmed and unhurt. The absurdity of this view is seen by the fact that we have reason to care about inequalities in the distribution of *goods* and *ills*, that is of what is of value or disvalue for independent reasons. There is no reason to care about inequalities in the distribution of grains of sand, unless there is some other reason to wish to have or to avoid sand.

Relational goods, or the principles that regulate them, accordingly, are never what ultimately matters in morality. It is, in any case, bizarre to suppose that a purely relational property could have intrinsic value. Moreover, egalitarianism, like other forms of distributionism, has a corrupting effect on our thought, since it distracts us from concern with what alone matters in political morality—namely, the well-being of individuals. As Raz has again put it:

> ... What makes us care about various inequalities is not the inequality but the concern identified by the underlying principle. It is the hunger of the hungry, the need of the needy, the suffering of the ill, and so on. The fact that they are worse off in the relevant respect than their neighbours is relevant. But it is relevant not as an independent evil of inequality. Its relevance is in showing that their hunger is greater, their need more pressing, their suffering more hurtful, and therefore our concern for the hungry, the needy, the suffering and not our concern for equality, makes us give them priority.

> ... Our concern for the suffering, the unhappy, the unfulfilled is greater the greater their suffering or unhappiness. We have no reason to stop and ask whether the gap between the unhappy person and the rest of humanity is great to justify or to quantify our concern for him. His suffering or unhappiness matter in themselves, and the greater they are the more they matter.[39]

Egalitarian political moralities have other absurd and offensive features. Consider the question of natural endowments—the abilities and talents we receive via the genetic lottery. It has never been explained satisfactorily by egalitarians why these should not be subject to redistribution. If one man is blind and another fully sighted, why not transfer one eye from the sighted to the blind man, so that both are then partially sighted? If, as seems obvious, the natural talents of people are sometimes decisive for their well-being, ought we not (on egalitarian principles) to tax those of superior natural abilities, so as to achieve a level playing field in society? The standard, conventional answer to these pertinent questions is that the pursuit of equality is reasonably constrained by other values, such as individual liberty and respect for human personality, which policies of redistribution of bodily parts, say, would violate. Common, indeed ubiquitous as this response is, it is extremely feeble. For policies which forcibly redistribute estates that have been in the hands of families for generations may have as injurious an impact on the liberties and personalities of the family members as any hypothetical policy for the redistribution of bodily parts might be expected to have. There is nothing in egalitarian morality that can in principle rule out the horribly dystopian society envisaged in L.P. Hartley's novel, *Facial Justice*,[40] in which the beautiful and the ugly are subject to mandatory facial surgery with the aim of assimilating them to the average or mediocrity in personal appearance.

Nor is it clear why financial assets, say, acquired in the lottery of the market, or the family lottery of inheritance, should have any different moral status from those acquired via the genetic lottery. Either both are liable to redistribution, or neither. On the view presented here, there is no defensible principle for the redistribution of either type of asset. The welfare benefits defended are defended, not by reference to any distributional principle, but instead by appeal to the well-being of their holders. When we institute welfare benefits for the congenitally handicapped, we are not seeking to compensate them for bad luck in the genetic lottery. (How would such compensation be calculated, anyway?) We are aiming to protect and promote their well-being. No distributional principle is at stake in these or similar policies. Egalitarian moralities which make distribution fundamental not only incur all the absurdities identified by Raz: they also obscure the real reasons why we help the unfortunate.

Egalitarian moralities also soon come up against an awkward institution—the family. As Hayek and Nozick, among others, have noted,[41] the good fortune of being born into a happy, civilised family is one that may prove decisive as to one's life chances. Quite apart from any question as to the propriety of inheritance of financial assets, the institution of the family is bound to confer very different inheritances of cultural or human capital on different children. It will also play a decisive role in sending them out into the world happy or sad, alert or insensitive, confident or hesitant. Whereas good (and, in part, state-funded) schooling ought to have as one of its aims the goal of enabling every child to make the best of his or her abilities, it cannot wholly undo whatever harm families may have already done. For this reason, egalitarian morality cannot be other than hostile to the institution of the family—a point that Plato (no egalitarian himself) recognised, but which most egalitarian theorizing has since suppressed. Egalitarians who are sufficiently intrepid as to entertain an assault on the family might care to scrutinize the evidence regarding the early socialist kibbutzim in Israel, which uniformly failed.[42] Egalitarianism suffers from the disadvantage of making impossible (as well as morally unacceptable) demands on us.

The proposal advanced here is that, rather than concern ourselves with any distributional principle, egalitarian or otherwise, conceived as foundational in political morality, we treat as foundational *satiable basic human needs*. These are human needs that are basic inasmuch as the satisfaction is a precondition of a worthwhile human life and they are satiable in that (unlike the pursuit of pleasure or power, say) their content can be fully met. The proposal is that guaranteeing the satisfaction of these needs—by an enabling welfare state, where the institutions of civil society cannot do so—is a fundamental principle of the same political morality, aimed at promoting autonomy, that grounds market institutions. Identifying basic needs and specifying resource levels for their provision is, on this account, a matter for rational public discourse, just like discourse about the allocation of resources for law and order and national defense in that it has an aspect of essential indeterminacy (but not, therefore, of arbitrariness). Like market institutions, an enabling welfare state dedicated to the satisfaction of basic needs is justified neither by its function as a maximiser of aggregate or collective welfare nor by any theory of rights or of justice, but instead by its contribution to human well-being, and in particular to that vital ingredient in human well-being we have specified as autonomy. As will later emerge, the fact that the enabling welfare state is justified by its impact on the individual human good is important, since it distinguishes it from any conception of welfare state that is distributionist, rights-based or justice-orientated. In *this* view, the welfare state is an enabling device for autonomy, different only in structure from market institutions; and, like market institutions, it facilitates not only the exercise of individual autonomy, but also the renewal of a voluntarist community. These are points to which I shall return.

Unlike, say, the classical utilitarian principle of maximizing pleasure, principles mandating the satiation of basic needs have the property of being *diminishing*, and they can always in principle be met completely. However much pleasure one has had, one may always have more; but once a basic need has been met, there is no reason for further action. Utilitarianism in morals and politics is to be rejected, among other reasons, because of the limitless and inexhaustible demands it puts upon us. Egalitarianism, along with other forms of distributionism, is to be rejected because it falsely attributes intrinsic value to relational properties that have none in themselves. It is a cardinal point in my argument, therefore, that the basic principles of political morality can be neither aggregative (having to do with collective or general welfare) nor distributive (having to do with comparative standing). They are instead, all of them, diminishing principles, having as their subject matter individual human well-being and the satisfaction of basic needs in respect of vital interests central to well-being.

Political morality—at least one that is in any sense liberal—can therefore be neither consequentialist nor distributionist in its foundation. That does not mean that it cannot be sensitive to consequences and distributions. Indeed the diminishing principles that mandate satisfaction of basic needs are themselves both consequence-sensitive and distribution-sensitive. They give guidance when resource-scarcity prevents the full satiation of the needs of all. They guide us to relieve the greater suffering rather than the lesser, to give medicine to those who would otherwise die rather than food to those who (though suffering from malnutrition) will survive, and so on. It may even be that a version of Rawls's Difference Principle, which enjoins that we ought to give priority to bettering the lot of the worst-off, should be adopted as a ruling maxim in social policy. If so, however, it would be as a rough rule of thumb, not as a matter of principle, and it would not arise from any distributionist concern. It would recognise (as Rawls does not) that the worst-off are a very heterogeneous bunch, not a single group, and that they have very different needs. And it would have no concern (as Rawls does) with lowering the maximum in society: its concern would solely be with the worst-off. It would thereby diverge radically from any fundamentalist egalitarian standpoint, even as it assigned priority to the needs of the neediest, and so was distribution-sensitive. The very principles that mandate satisfaction of basic needs enjoin us to satisfy the most urgent needs when all cannot be fully satiated. They thereby deviate from the straight maximising objective of utilitarian ethics—even if, on occasion, when resources are scarce and satiable needs commensurable, policy may unavoidably, and rightly, have a utilitarian dimension. They are for these reasons consequence-sensitive (but not consequentialist) principles.

Similarly, these principles will take note of distributions insofar as these are relevant to the project of satisfying basic needs. A policy of paying nursing home fees for all who need such care, regardless of their income or capital or other resources, would be massively wasteful, and would yield a level of care that would be unacceptably low. Accordingly, it is reasonable to target such benefits, as at present in Britain, to those whose income or capital is nonexistent, small or exhausted (I leave aside here the precise mix of criteria that ought to be invoked to assess needs for targeting purposes—should it count capital or the income from capital, or some compound of the two?—as not being material to the substance of my argument.) Such a policy of targeting the disability welfare benefits of the sorts under consideration at this point is inherent in our concern for the efficacy of the right itself. Although they are not distributionist, the principles underlying welfare rights are in this way distribution-sensitive.

The importance of distribution is always contingent or subsidiary, never primordial or fundamental. What is objectionable in egalitarianism is what is wrong with every form of distributionism—its fixation on relational qualities that have no moral status. As Hayek has noted,[43] the very concern to impose a pattern on distribution is illiberal, in that it can only distort the constantly changing patterns produced by free individual choices. Governments may be concerned about distribution, and may have policies to affect it—policies aiming to discourage excessive concentrations of wealth and to encourage its wide dispersal. These will be policies motivated, not by justice, but by other values, such as communal harmony and the enlargement of opportunity.

Distributionism has corrupted our thought by focusing not on individuals in themselves but on their relative positions. It has introduced into thought and practice a corrosive spirit of comparison which has obscured our perception of what is truly good and bad in human lives. Recent liberal thought has been fettered by the distributionist dogma that justice is the first virtue of social institutions. This may be so, but only in the Millian sense that it protects certain utilities, interests or goods that are vital to a worthwhile human life.[44] A worthwhile human life can be lived, as has long been recognised, at least since Aristotle, only in a community that is itself rich, sound and harmonious in its practices. The virtue of justice—in a society, an economy or a polity—is never primordial, in that it always presupposes, as one of its necessary conditions, a host of other virtues in a common culture. When justice is conceived, as it often is in recent liberal and libertarian ideology, as a virtue appropriate to those who have nothing else in common, it is being theorized as a virtue for a society of strangers that, in real historical practice, would be unlikely to last much longer than a generation. In real historical terms, justice in human institutions always depends on the resources of a common life, and is weakened as these are depleted. Justice is a virtue of common procedures—the virtue of fairness—not of substantive outcomes.

We may rightly concern ourselves with the endowments people have when they enter the market; but, when we do so, we do not invoke the imaginary claims of social justice, but rather the preconditions of individual well-being and of a stable and harmonious community.[45] The bottom line in political morality is thus never justice or rights, but instead the individual well-being they protect and the common culture in which it is realised.

Egalitarian distributionism is, from a point of view that is genuinely liberal, perhaps one of the worst forms of distributionism. In practice, it often amounts to little more than the 'anti-social envy'[46] that Mill presciently condemned among his contemporaries. Again, the rhetoric of social justice in which egalitarian demands are framed often serves merely to give a moral rationale to entrenched interests. In real political life, it is not the submerged and defenceless elements of the population—the disabled, the chronically sick, or the long-term unemployed, for example—who are the focus of attention of those who speak of social justice. It is instead the professional and middle classes, who already do best from the welfare state. The egalitarian rhetoric of social justice thereby has, in actual political practice, the perverse functions of curbing healthy alterations in relative incomes in society and of distracting attention from the lot of the truly unfortunate. Worst, egalitarianism suppresses the vital truth that, if the really unfortunate are to be assisted by redistribution, it will have to be by a redistribution from the affluent majority, and not from the rich minority (whose wealth would be insufficient to the task, even if it could be transferred without loss). The real effect of egalitarianism in political life in western democracies, accordingly, is to generate pernicious illusions about the potential benefits of redistribution from the rich, while doing nothing to enhance the opportunities of the disadvantaged, or to alleviate the lot of the needy.

Because it neglects merits and deserts, egalitarianism is especially inimical to liberty and responsibility. It dissociates the rewards people receive from their actions, and so nullifies the moral importance of their actions. Note that, by recognising the importance of merit and desert, we are *not* thereby arguing that the distribution of resources in society as a whole should correspond to these moral values. For, as Hayek has noted, people's merits and deserts are difficult to know, except in very limited contexts, and are surely unknowable by governments. Again, even if merit and desert were knowable, allocating resources according to them would have massive disincentive effects and a devastating impact on the self-esteem of those judged undeserving or unmeritorious.[47] For many reasons, of which the epistemic problem is the most important and least appreciated, the ideal of allocating resources across the whole of society according to such moral criteria is a foolish one. The objection to egalitarianism depends, not on such a distributionist ideal, but on the complete severance of rewards from personal conduct which egalitarianism would effect. As Hayek has put it, the market is akin to poker, a game of skill and chance.[48] The objection to egalitarianism is that, in removing the elements of both skill and chance from the allocation of resources in society, it would destroy market institutions. Or, to put the point the other way around: accepting market institutions involves accepting an unpredictable dispersion of rewards that is only partly connected with anyone's merits or deserts. It is this partial or imperfect connection that egalitarianism would destroy.

Proposals for the equalisation of resources among people fail to recognise, where they do not actively suppress, the vital truth that virtually all the resources and wealth in a modern society are the result of human action, not manna from heaven. The egalitarian idea that production and distribution are radically separable activities, first advanced by J.S. Mill,[49] expresses the extraordinary delusion that human actions will proceed as before, even when their outcomes have been thoroughly distorted by a distributional programme on egalitarian lines. In truth, an egalitarian regime in which rewards bear no relation with human action would be one in which (if it could be achieved) human responsibility had been altogether extinguished. In practice, egalitarian policies invariably generate a corrupt, inefficient and often exploitative parallel economy, in which human responsibility survives only in a compromised and degraded form. Ultimately, it is the logic of egalitarianism to collectivise responsibility for individual actions—and thereby to destroy it.

Finally, as de Jouvenel points out in his unjustly neglected study,[50] the political result of distributionism in its egalitarian variety is to effect an ever-greater socialisation of income. It is one of the many ironies of egalitarianism that, in aiming to reduce the economic inequalities thrown up in market economies, it should create vast inequalities in political power—political inequalities that (as in the communist regimes) soon reproduce themselves as economic inequalities often greater than those in market societies.[51] History and experience teach us that, incoherent as it is in philosophical terms, egalitarianism has in practice the signal inconvenience of being self-defeating.

Egalitarianism lacks philosophical credibility and, in practical terms, is felled by the same epistemic and incentive problems that defeat socialist central planning. Let us see if market socialism can escape these results of our argument so far.

5

The Blind Alley of Market Socialism

The argument so far has been that, whereas unconstrained libertarian capitalism cannot be justified by moral arguments, egalitarianism is in no stronger a position. The principled position appears to be that which grounds the market economy in its contribution to autonomy as a vital ingredient in individual well-being and which (as I shall next argue in greater detail) invokes precisely the same value to ground an enabling welfare state. It might be argued, however, that the defence of the market economy so far developed does not justify market capitalism, since it is acceptable to market socialists. By market socialism is meant here, not the simulation of market pricing by central planning institutions theorized in the Lange-Lerner model, devastatingly criticised by Hayek,[52] but instead the model of an economic system in which the private ownership of the means of production has been abolished and replaced by a system of communal or collective ownership by worker-cooperatives which stand to each other in relations of market competition. Market socialism so conceived, and as advocated most ably in Britain by David Miller,[53] is to be distinguished not only from the simulated markets of the Lange-Lerner model, but also from the 'competitive syndicalism' of J.S. Mill and from egalitarian social democracy. It differs from Millian competitive syndicalism in that the worker-cooperatives that Mill envisaged as ultimately supplanting capitalist firms were to be voluntarily instituted and were conceived as forms of producer cooperation in which the shares of individual workers were individually owned, and could therefore freely be alienated, by them.[54] In the model theorized by Miller and other market socialists, the collective ownership of productive assets by the worker cooperative precludes individual workers selling off their shares, or, at the very least, it prohibits the reinvestment of such shares in other worker-cooperatives of which the worker is not a member. The constitutive feature of market socialism in this model is, accordingly, in the fusion of job-holding with capital ownership, and, in consequence, in the prohibition of wage-labour and of a market in worker's assets in their cooperatives. Market socialism on this model is, finally, to be distinguished from Swedish-style egalitarian social democracy, in which an extensive redistributional and welfarist apparatus was superimposed (with considerable damage to incentives) on classical capitalist economic institutions.

It is evident that, in the model so presented, there is market pricing of all or most assets, including labour, but not of capital. Although market socialist schemes come in a variety of forms, it is a feature of all of them that capital is allocated to the worker-cooperatives by state investment banks, not by private investors, institutional or personal. It is at this point that the objections to worker-cooperatives on Austrian and Virginian lines emerge. As we noted in Chapter One, it is a fundamental objection to central planning that the planners will in the absence of market pricing inevitably lack the knowledge of relative scarcities needed for rational resource-allocation. It is for this reason that centrally planned economic systems are endemically wasteful and riddled with mal-investments and other allocative inefficiencies. The question now arises: if market pricing is a precondition of rationality in the allocation of all other assets and resources, why is not the same true of capital? In other words, without a capital market, how can the state investment banks know what are the most productive uses of the investment capital at their disposal? This is, it is worth reminding ourselves, an epistemic argument against market socialism that depends in no way on any assumptions regarding the motives or the incentives of the state investment bankers. The argument is merely a further application, in a very important specific context, of the epistemic case against central planning. Its policy implication is a radical one, undercutting a constitutive feature of market socialism in all its varieties. The policy implication is that there be a market in capital—which is to say, private or several ownership of capital. At this point, we are at least half-way towards the reinvention of one of the key institutions of market capitalism, or at least of the institution of a free market in private or several property in the means of production which market socialism sought to suppress.

Though the epistemic argument is the deepest and most fundamental one against socialism in all its forms, including market socialism, it needs to be supplemented by the incentive argument as theorized in the Virginia School of Public Choice. The incentive argument applies, in the first instance, to the state investment banks themselves. Since they lack the information for the rational allocation of capital, by what criteria or procedures will they distribute it? Why, in particular, should they not be highly risk-averse and conservative of their capital assets? If the answer is that there ought to be a plurality of such banks, competing with each other as profitable enterprises then, once again, we are now well beyond half-way down the path of reinventing a central institution of private property and the free market. This will be especially so, if, in order to give the various banks an incentive to pursue profits, an element of the profit accrues to the state investment bankers themselves. This is tantamount to a partial reinstitution of private banking and is unlikely to be a stable institutional arrangement.

The second level at which incentive arguments apply is at the level of the worker-cooperative itself. Existing worker-cooperatives will have an incentive to engage in a political competition for capital from the state investment banks. In this competition, it is virtually inevitable that existing, well-established worker-cooperatives will have a structural advantage over those that are new and speculative—and, above all, over those that are at present just a gleam in an entrepreneurial eye. It is to be expected, for this reason, that the allocation of capital under market socialist institutions will replicate the disabling inefficiencies of straightforward central planning institutions: it will favour entrenched producer groups, exhibit a high degree of risk aversion and a tendency to seek to conceal mal-investments. In none of these respects is market socialism a significant improvement on socialism as theorized and practised in the terms of a command economy.

The structure of worker-cooperatives will also generate perverse incentives within them. Since job-holding and capital-ownership are fused, there will be an incentive for the worker-cooperatives to limit entry to the enterprise—in practice, often to relatives—since every extra worker dilutes the share of the rest in the enterprise's capital. Moreover, there will be an incentive slowly to consume the capital of the enterprise, rather than to invest it in risky research and development schemes, for example, since the enterprise always has the option of replenishing its capital fund by turning for help to the state investment bank. It is difficult to envisage a workable set of institutions that would prevent this upshot, since the only one we know for a surety that prevents, or inhibits, this tendency to slow capital-consumption is the traditional sanction of bankruptcy. Were this to be introduced, we would be yet further down the slippery slope towards the full-scale reinvention of the institutions of private property and the free market. In fact, the policy implication for the worker-cooperative enterprise of the incentive argument is that its dynamic efficiency is likely to be enhanced, only if the worker-cooperators are fully liable to the risks of a policy of stagnation. This, in turn, will be so, only if worker-cooperators have the freedom to exit from the enterprise, taking with them their share of the capital assets. At this point, however, we are witnessing the reinvention of private property in the means of production—albeit in one of its least developed forms, that of the private family firm. If we have gone this far, under the compulsion provided by the incoherences and perverse incentives of a system of worker-cooperatives, it is unclear why we should not go the whole way, and allow fully alienable and marketable private ownership of the means of production.

The shortcomings of market socialism that are derivable from its theoretical model are fully corroborated by the evidences of the Yugoslav experiment now manifestly at an end.[55] This is a system that has exhibited massive structural unemployment, technological stagnation, a chaotic political auction of capital and recurrent episodes of authoritarian intervention by the central government to prevent or redirect the abuses of the worker-cooperatives. All the empirical evidence supports, what the theoretical model itself implies, that market socialism is an unhappy halfway house between socialist central planning and the key implications of market capitalism. Economically highly inefficient, it is likely to be politically transitional, sustainable only under conditions of less than complete democratic political practice. Once again, the Yugoslav experience confirms this, disclosing that, as the communist state disintegrates to be replaced by varieties of popular democracy, market socialism will vanish down the memory hole of history, unremembered and unlamented by the workers who have been subject to its inefficiencies and inequities.

It remains to consider what are the positive arguments for market socialism, given its considerable theoretical and practical failings. We may, I think, justly set aside arguments from exploitation and alienation as distinctive or peculiar features of capitalist institutions. Either these arguments invoke conceptions of exploitation and alienation that derive from classical Marxism, or they rest upon empirical claims about the actual circumstances and preferences of workers. It is an unambiguous result of recent philosophical inquiry, including that of the school of analytical Marxism,[56] that classical Marxist conceptions of alienation and exploitation are indefensible, depending as they do on untenable doctrines such as the labour theory of value and an Hegelian account of human nature that is not translatable in ordinary empirical terms. On the other hand, if we look instead at the empirical realities of the lives of workers—their bargaining power vis-a-vis their employers, their attitudes to the jobs, and so forth—nothing whatever supports the view that the sense of estrangement or exploitation is reduced under socialist institutions. If anything, the opposite appears to be the case. Nor does it matter much whether the institutions are those of centralist command-style socialism or those of market socialist worker-cooperatives. Under the latter, the institutions and practices of self-management are diluted by the inevitable emergence of managerial elites and curtailed by frequent episodes of authoritarian intervention (in investment and hiring policy, for example) by central government. There is not a shred of empirical evidence that most workers prefer self-managed worker-cooperatives to capitalist corporations, or that they would not choose to exit from the former to the latter if they had the choice.

A complex counter-argument to that sketched above has been developed by David Miller.[57] Miller's argument is exceptional in acknowledging the problems of under-investment generated by the incentive structure of worker-cooperatives and in accepting that there is little, if any, real evidence of widespread demand for producer cooperatives or even for employee participation. However, Miller seeks to explain these observed facts, or at least to resist their normative force and implications, by invoking the idea that worker-cooperatives in a predominantly capitalist environment find themselves in a Prisoner's Dilemma whereby they cannot flourish competitively, or, in the end and for the most part, even survive. The problem of under-investment alone, which worker-cooperatives face, condemns most of them to extinction. More subtly, but according to Miller no less pervasively and effectively, a capitalist economic environment will bias workers' preferences to income-maximization as distant from other, unobtainable goals (such as job-satisfaction or workplace participation). The upshot of Miller's argument is that a minimalist state in which most assets are embodied in capitalist institutions is not, as Nozick claimed it to be, *neutral* with respect to the form of productive enterprise its citizens elect to engage in. Instead, because the intending worker-cooperators are in a Prisoner's Dilemma which condemns most of their projects to extinction in a capitalist environment, we must say that they are *discriminated against* in the circumstances Miller and Nozick have specified. The result of Miller's argument, as he himself candidly acknowledges, is that if worker-cooperation or market socialism is ever to come about, it can only do so if the state intervenes and (in Nozick's famous expression) forbids capitalist acts among consenting adults.[58]

Miller's ingenious argument fails. It is true, as he says, that worker-cooperatives will on the whole fare badly in a capitalist environment. On this point market socialists and market liberals have no reason for disagreement. But does this failure show the non-neutrality of the legal framework of a liberal state? Or suggest that worker-cooperatives, or the ideal of worker-cooperation, has been discriminated against? It does not, for at least three reasons. Firstly, the neutrality of the liberal state is bound to be limited.[59] No liberal state can afford to legitimate, or to tolerate, practices (such as slavery, serfdom or enforced marriage) that violate the central norms of a liberal civil society. It is open to the critic of worker-cooperation to maintain that a system of worker-cooperatives of the sort Miller advocates violates the legitimate freedom of the worker who, after due consideration, decides that he wishes to work for a capitalist corporation. What justifies the coercive interdiction of the worker's choice? Why is the conscription of the unwilling worker into a worker-cooperative (or his marginalisation into self-employment or public service) more justifiable than his impressment into serfdom?) As Gaus has well put it:

> Worker managed market socialist firms certainly can reward workers differentially, recognizing the differential claims to the fruits of labour, but market socialism in effect expropriates the earnings of workers invested in their firms. If, as Mill said, one has a claim to the fruits of his abstinence, market socialism tends systematically to ignore this. Workers who have heavily invested, especially older workers, have no exclusionary rights to these funds, entirely losing them on leaving the firm.[60]

The effect of market socialism on workers is, in short, to imprison them in their worker-cooperatives, where they may be subject to exploitative interference by central government. It is difficult to see what advantage such an arrangement has (from the point of view of the worker) over the more straightforward and transparent exploitation of workers' labour practised in socialist command economies.

A second objection to Miller's argument is that it accords an undefended privilege to the ideal of worker-cooperatives. It is true, as I have already observed, that capitalist economies tend to drive out worker-cooperatives. But they also tend to drive out other forms of productive enterprise that embody ideals that are incompatible with those of market socialism. The small corner shop is as threatened by capitalist competition as the worker-cooperative. The family firm, especially when it is also small, does not often last for many generations. Capitalist economies make life difficult for those with the ideal of productive enterprise harboured by early, pioneering capitalist managers and free-wheeling entrepreneurs. Is the liberal state (within which capitalist institutions are dominant) thereby discriminatory, or non-neutral with regard to these other ideals of productive life? If not, Miller needs to explain why its adverse impact on worker-cooperatives amounts to discriminatory non-neutrality when its undermining impact on such other ideals is discounted. It is difficult to avoid the conclusion that, the moral appeal of market socialism appearing self-evident to Miller, he proceeds to project it onto workers, who in practice care nothing for it, or resist it because of its clear disadvantages for them.

The third point follows naturally from the first two. If Miller has any good reason to accord a privileged position to the ideal of worker-cooperation, it must be that he supposes there to be a submerged preference in its favour among the workers. It is hard to see why he supposes this. It is true, as he says,[61] that there is some evidence, albeit rather inconclusive, pointing to a preference among workers for greater participation in managerial decision-making. This is far from constituting a considered judgement in favour of a fundamental change in economic systems. On the one hand, evidence from progressive capitalist enterprises (such as Volvo) suggests that much of this dissatisfaction can be met within the context of capitalist institutions. On the other hand, there are good reasons for supposing that, even supposing (contrary to all available indicators) there were a significant, submerged body of worker opinion in favour of a shift to worker-cooperatives, it would dwindle or vanish once the economic costs of such a shift became evident to workers.

The costs would be massive, and would come in various forms, some of them recognised by Miller himself. Large economies of scale would have to be sacrificed if the economy were to be broken down into small, participatory units. The benefits of the international division of labour would be compromised to the extent that such a fragmentation occurred within a nation-state. (Would there be market socialism in one country? Would transnational corporations be forbidden to operate upon market socialist soil, or to invest in worker-cooperatives?)[62] The costs of production in a market socialist system would, almost inevitably, be higher than in capitalist corporations, and so the resultant prices would be higher, too. Would a nation-state that had opted for market socialism protect its worker-cooperatives, by tariffs and subsidies, against competition from foreign capitalist corporations? If so, reduced living standards would very likely follow. The evidence is that, for these reasons and because of endemic under investment, worker cooperatives would under-perform capitalist corporations even where the latter had in a particular nation been rendered illegal. The prospect for a nation-state that adopts market socialism is that of falling living standards and of increasing isolation from the global economy. It is difficult to see this as a prospect workers will welcome, or as one they are prepared to accept as the price for an ideal that few of them even avow or prize.

In world-historical terms, market socialism is in any case an anachronism. If in Western societies there is an absence of any political force in its favour, in the post-communist countries it has been abandoned and rejected, both by workers and by the ruling elites, as a utopian third way between market capitalism and socialist planning. In the former Soviet bloc, when market socialism is not treated with indifference, it is rejected with derision. It is hard not to endorse de Jasay's verdict that '... non-private ownership is a core requirement of market socialism, and genuine markets must somehow prove to be compatible with it. It is the pivotal place of this doctrine that really differentiates market socialism from the bankrupt doctrine of orthodox and, as I would insist, genuine socialism, as well as from the ad hoc compromises of social democracy'.[63] Theoretically indefensible, market socialist institutions are in practice systemically unstable, tending to revert to central planning or to mutate into something resembling market capitalism. Wherever political democracy is instituted, the tendency to the latter is virtually irresistible.

Having been removed by the force of events from the agenda of history, it is high time that market socialism be struck off the agenda of policy. At most, the real spectrum of political discourse now extends from unconstrained libertarian capitalism to egalitarian social democracy, with both ends of the spectrum accepting the core institutions of private property and free markets in most productive assets. Market socialism is little more than a distraction from this emergent consensus.

Nothing said so far is meant to imply that existing capitalist institutions are to be endorsed in their current forms, which are a product of historical accident and may well be appropriate subjects of reform. As a long tradition of liberal thought has always stressed, the corporation as we know it is an artifact of law, a legal fiction whose powers and immunities are open to criticism, reform, and amendment.[64] Again, the form of unencumbered property rights that Honore identifies as liberal ownership[65] is in the real world of law almost a limiting case with the law allowing a variety of forms of variously encumbered property rights. Yet again, the pattern of contractual liberties and immunities which characterises current western capitalist institutions is not necessary or inevitable, but may be inappropriate in many contexts, and in need of reform as it stands in the West. Finally, and perhaps most importantly, there is no convincing reason to suppose that the model of the Western capitalist corporation will be the most appropriate one in the emergent post-communist societies or should be copied everywhere in the world. A policy of privatisation on the Western model presupposes, in most of these societies, and especially in Russia, a law of property and a tradition of legal corporate personality that either never existed, or which has been comprehensively destroyed. It may be that, as James Buchanan has argued in a seminal paper, what is needed in Russia is not the transposition there of Western capitalist institutions, but instead a *radical deconcentration* of economic power,[66] in which private property and market exchange are reinstituted at village, cooperative and municipal levels. (Freeing up the parallel economy, alongside deconcentration of the state sector, is likely to be another necessary measure.) If this is so, then an agrarian capitalism of cooperatives, together with something akin to Millian competitive syndicalism in industry (incorporating the vital freedom of the workers to exit from the cooperative with his capital that market socialism denies) may well be a far better prospect for the reinstitution of a market economy in Russia than the (probably futile) attempt to import the standard institutions of Western capitalism. Again, the Western, and particularly the American project of forcing liberalisation on a Western model on Japanese economic institutions, may well be thoroughly misconceived, neglecting the embeddedness of Japanese economic life in a distinctive and highly resilient culture. To recognise this is to acknowledge that, whereas market socialism is an unworkable absurdity, free markets can be combined with a variety of form of ownership, and do not flourish only within the institutions of Western corporate capitalism.

In any modern state, forms of property rights will be pluralistic and diverse, fitting badly with any single theory or doctrine. In any modern Western state, no doubt, the dominant form of economic enterprise will be the capitalist corporation. It, too, however, comes in a variety of shapes, and may properly be the subject of reform (by the encouragement of employee share-holding, and other devices, for example). With all of these qualifications and variations, it is in the acceptance of the core institutions of the market economy—the institutions of private property and voluntary exchange—rather than in the deluded pursuit of the mirage of market socialism—a mirage long dispelled in the post-communist lands—that progress, intellectual, economic and political, is to be found.

6

An Enabling Welfare State

It has been the argument so far that market institutions are best defended as enabling devices for individual autonomy. The argument now being advanced is that the same considerations of individual autonomy which justify market institutions over real-world alternatives mandate the institution of an enabling welfare state—a state, that is to say, which confers on people a variety of claims to goods, services and resources. Before proceeding with the substantive argument for the institution of such a welfare state, it may be worth briefly setting out in the most general terms the structure and content of such a welfare state. It would aim to provide a guarantee of the resources and opportunities required for the autonomous pursuit of the good life, where these are not provided, or are under-provided, by the institutions of civil society—by the spontaneously formed groupings of family, neighbourhood and community, by private self-provision and by charitable agencies. The argument here is that, having given full scope to these elements of civil life, there remains in any modern state such as Britain an indispensable and vital role for government in the funding (but not always or most desirably, the provision) of welfare benefits, aimed at the satisfaction of basic needs. The structure of an enabling welfare state would, because of the complexity of human needs and the environment of incentives which welfare institutions (like market institutions) create, inevitably be pluralist. It would encompass universal provision, as with the National Health Service and, perhaps, the basic state retirement pension; benefits aimed at reintegrating, or integrating for the first time, people into the market economy and civil life, which should typically carry with them correlative obligations; and a variety of benefits for those incapable of full productive life in the economy, such as the disabled, which do not carry with them correlative obligations but are targeted with reference to the recipients' capital and income, and which, in having the status of entitlements (subject to the relevant criteria) are akin to welfare rights. The justification of this pluralist mix of welfare policies and institutions is the same as that of market institutions—the promotion of individual well-being and, more particularly, of autonomous choice among the worthwhile options provided by a rich and deep community. It is in these terms, and not in the terms of justice or rights, that the enabling welfare state is to be defended. It is important that the rejection of a rights based defence of the welfare state advanced here not be confused with the objections to welfare rights that are part of the received conventional wisdom of latter-day classical liberals.

These objections are well summarized by Norman Barry.[67] Welfare rights, unlike the traditional negative, passive liberal rights against coercion and force, demand more than the non-interference of others for their protection: they impose obligations on others to act to supply goods and services. Further, welfare rights are extremely sensitive to resource-scarcity and conflicts among them can easily arise: welfare rights therefore do not possess the property of non-conflictability or compossibility[68] held by negative rights against aggression. As a related point, welfare rights are highly indeterminate, their content being under-determined by any easily ascertainable body of hard empirical fact. (Is it a matter of objective or empirical fact, the critic of welfare rights asks, what are a person's medical needs?) For this last reason, welfare rights are not easily justiciable. And, since they presuppose a level of wealth that is historically rare, they cannot claim the property of universality that is usually associated with basic rights. In view of the fact that welfare rights do not possess the properties of non-conflictability and consequent peremptoriness or non-over-ridability possessed by negative rights, nor the determinacy of content and universality that are commonly attributed to the classical liberal negative rights against aggression, the critic of welfare rights concludes that there is a deep moral asymmetry between negative rights and welfare rights, such that the latter are not really rights at all, but at best perhaps ideals or expressions of benevolence.

None of these arguments has any significant force. Negative rights, like welfare rights, impose obligations on others and make demands on resources in any real world in which rights are not afforded protection, by the enforcement of sanctions for their violation.. A minimum state, concerned solely with national defence and the enforcement of the criminal and civil law, might still be enormously large, devouring up much of the wealth of society.[69] Not only does the protection of negative rights demand the appropriation by the state of scarce resources, it is also true that there may be competition and conflict among negative rights in their claims upon resources. Switching police manpower from street patrols to anti-terrorist activities may save lives but result in an increase in muggings. Negative rights are no more compossible, that is, no less likely to conflict with each other, in the real world than are welfare rights. Again, the obligations imposed by negative rights are not always ones of forbearance. Jury service, and military conscription, as well as the obligation to pay taxes to support the minimum state, are all positive actions, constraining the negative liberty and appropri-ating some of the resources of the citizen. Finally, all rights are conditional: rights to life or liberty may be withdrawn, over-ridden, or forfeited by imprisonment or capital punishment if their holder's conduct justifies such abridgment. In all these respects, negative rights and welfare rights enjoy full moral parity.

The classical liberal defence of negative rights, like its defence of negative liberty, depends upon a number of disabling illusions. Consider the claim that specifying the content of welfare rights come up against problems of determinacy. Is this not also, and equally, the case with specifying the content of negative rights? No one who knows anything of the legal history and jurisprudence of the supposed rights to property, to privacy or to freedom of information can suppose that their content is easily determined, or conflicts among them simply arbitrated. The easy justiciability of negative rights is merely a seductive mirage, generated not by anything in the real world of law, but the product of a theory that is insulated from the uncertainties, indeterminacies and endemic hard cases with which real law abounds. The universality of negative rights is no less delusive. They sometimes compete with each other, such that not all can be protected, and their content is often significantly culture-specific. (What counts as rape in other cultures and other jurisdictions? What murder?) There may be something akin to the minimum content of natural law, theorized by H.L.A. Hart,[70] but it is doubtful in the extreme if this can be given a content statable in a determinate list of universal negative rights.

We may, then, dismiss these commonplace objections to the discourse of welfare rights, and proceed to consider their true objections to the discourse of rights in general. At this point it is well that a few remarks are made on the very notion of a right. As Raz has shown,[71] rights are never fundamental or primordial in political discourse or political morality. Claims about rights are intermediary or conclusionary claims about the relations between the interests central to the well-being of persons and the obligations generated upon others by these interests. There is then an ineradicable open-texture (*not* avoidable in other theories) about the discourse of rights, negative *or* positive. The content or contours of any alleged right are shaped by our knowledge of the vital interests, or the conditions of well-being, of the persons under consideration. This is to say that, in political and in moral philosophy, the good is always prior to the right: we make judgments about the rights people have, only on the basis of our judgment of the interests central to their well-being. The project of a purely deontic theory of rights—that is to say, one which appeals only to principles of justice or the right, and which does not invoke any particular conception of the good life—is bound to founder, as it does in Kant and Gewirth, in the no-man's land between contentlessness and foundationlessness. All the content that rights may have, and all their ethical weight, derives, in short, from their contribution to vital human interests.

The dependency of rights on their contribution to individual well-being gives the clue as to the true limitations of rights discourse in respect to government and the welfare state. For, in the first place, the conditions of well-being are too diverse, too subtle and too variable to be captured in the thin and rigid discourse of rights. Individual well-being depends on a host of conditions, including decent cultural traditions and rich forms of common life, which the theory of rights cannot address nor the practice of rights guarantee. Autonomy, as a vital ingredient in well-being, cannot be guaranteed by any structure of rights, since it too depends on a matrix of cultural traditions and of communal life which rights cannot assure. Although, as I shall argue, there are classes of welfare benefit that ought to have the status of entitlements if they are to promote or respect auton- omy, and so are akin to welfare rights, the goal of enhancing autonomy demands a pluralist mixture of institutions and policies that cannot be squeezed into the Procrustean contours of rights theory.

There are other, no less fundamental objections to the discourse of rights in its application both to government in general and to the welfare state. The discourse of rights is in its nature universalistic and monolithic. If there are any rights at all, it would seem that they are universal and immutable, possessed by all, once and for all. The implication of Raz's analysis, however, is that rights are variable and mutable, their scope and content waxing and waning as the conditions of individual well-being change. On the view advanced here, the discourse of rights is reducible to that of individual well-being, and is for that reason redundant. Moreover, the discourse of rights has the danger that it suggests that the best governmental and welfare initiatives and policies are (at least in principle) always the same. The view presented here, on the contrary, is that the conditions of human well-being are many and various, that they change and have only a few common elements (such as the importance of autonomy to human well-being in modern societies.) If the conditions of well-being are complex and variable in this way, it would seem folly to try to comprise them in any structure of rights.

The conditions of human well-being are, then, highly complex and changeable; but they may also be conflicting and competi- tive in their claims and in their demands on resources. This enables us to state yet another objection to the discourse of rights. The legalist discourse and practice of rights is peremp- tory and does not allow the trade-offs and compromises that are the stuff of political (and moral) life. When rights come into conflict with each other, they cannot be balanced: one must be overridden, or even extinguished, by the other. The theory and practice of rights conceals the fact, otherwise self-evident, that political life, like moral life, is a choice among necessary evils, as well as among uncombinable goods. It also acts as a recipe for intractable conflict among rival ideals and interests. The treatment of abortion as a matter of fundamental constitutional right rather than of legislative policy and possible compromise, makes of that issue an insoluble dilemma, hostile to civil peace. If rights are eliminated from political discourse, then a settlement can sometimes be reached on such issues that is stable because it is perceived as fair, even if no party to it is wholly satisfied with it. The effect of rights-discourse is to render political conflicts non-negotiable.

Nothing thus far advanced here is meant to suggest that rights have no place at all in political life. An institution such as the European Convention on Human Rights may be worth incorporating into British law as a summary of the various practices and procedures in which important civil liberties are embodied. It is as a conventional abridgement of the practices of civil society, however, and not as a theory of fundamental rights, that such institutions should figure in political life. The hegemony of the discourse of rights in political life has among its consequences, a culture of endemic legalism and the political corruption of law—as in the United States. Rather than attempting to fix political discourse within the illusory constraints of legalism, we are on firmer ground if we direct political discourse towards the conditions of individual well-being, the content of basic needs and the depth and limits of the common culture, and the inherently public goods it contains.

The use of the rhetoric of right in the context of welfare institutions, though it has leverage in important areas of policy, is in general inappropriate. For it inclines us to form welfare policy and institutions on the model of a theory of justice, with all its distributionist and universalist preoccupations, whereas the animating values of an enabling welfare state should be values of autonomy, human solidarity and community. A society in which there is an abandoned underclass, in which the frail and the ill are left to their own devices and lack organised assistance, governmental as well as private, is ignoble, unlovely and graceless, whether or not it violates any specifiable precept of justice. A society in which the poor lack dignity, in which those whom catastrophe has struck are left to their own devices, is not worth living in, regardless of whether it exemplifies the virtue of justice that is the shibboleth of liberal philosophy. In truth, the liberal claim for justice that it is the first and supreme virtue of social institutions is a piece of hubris. Justice is a far humbler affair, an artefact of the common life, a remedial virtue in which unfairness is corrected, and it is essentially procedural in character. Justice designates a set of reciprocities whereby we achieve a *modus vivendi*, not an ideal specified in terms of rigorist principles. It is true of some welfare benefits, I shall maintain, that they should be entrenched in entitlements governed by rules, and it is in general true that discretionary allocation of benefits will be perceived as arbitrary, so that considerations of fairness will arise in the first case and will tell against the latter. The model for an enabling welfare state is not, however, any theory of justice, if there can indeed be such a thing, but instead the preconditions of individual autonomy and rich community, with all their variations over time and across cultures. There is no one set of policies, no one structure of institutions, in which an enabling welfare state is best embodied. There is instead a diversity of local settlements, never final and always provisional, in which conflicting claims are given a temporary reconciliation, and the values of autonomy and community are accorded a more or less complete embodiment and expression. The enabling state is defended, accordingly, not as a dictate of justice (whatever that may be), but as a precondition of the good life.

At this point in the argument we need to return to the notion of a basic need, and to put to work Raz's seminal exploration[72] of the *satiability* of most basic needs. A *basic need*, as I shall understand it, is one whose satisfaction is essential to the possibility of a worthwhile life, and whose frustration renders impossible the living of a good life. For us, at least, autonomy is a basic need, whose deprivation curtails our prospects of a good life. Basic needs encompass needs whose satisfaction contributes to, or enhances autonomy, such as needs for food, housing, medical care, education and so forth. As I have noted, the satisfaction of these basic needs may be demanded as a condition of a worthwhile life, even if the life that is then lived fails to be very autonomous (as in the case of the Alzheimer's patient, say). This suggests that the claim to the satisfaction of a basic need may be over-determined in its justification on the ground that any welfare claim may promote several vital interests at the same time, including that upon which I mostly focus, the vital interest in autonomy.

The claim that is being advanced here is that an enabling welfare state provides for the satisfaction of basic needs. This claim must at once be qualified in a variety of ways. In a liberal civil society, it is, or ought to be, taken for granted that, for most people most of the time, the satisfaction of basic needs is a matter of personal responsibility. There is no persuasive ethical justification for the massive, over-extended welfare states of most modern societies, which often involve perverse redist-ributions to the middle classes (a process which is, however, not at all easy to reverse under democratic institutions). The welfare state being defended here, though more sensitive to the needs of the worst off, is more restrictive than most that exist in contemporary states.

Further, it is intended to come into operation when the resources of civil society are exhausted or inadequate. Much welfare provision will always occur in the context of sponta-neously occurring social groups—families, neighbourhoods, churches, friendships, and so on. Again, much that is presently done by governmental agencies could be devolved to private self-provision. Finally charitable agencies will always have an important role to play in welfare provision. In each of these three areas, the vitality of civil society could be strengthened by the extension of existing tax reliefs—to families and other similar groups, to voluntary schemes for self-provision, and to charities. Such extension and development of tax deductibility would go against the neo-liberal dogma of the neutrality of the 'level playing field' in tax policy—but that is no fault in it. At the same time, it would be the height of folly to suppose that such desirable measures could circumvent the necessity of government funding and (in some instances) provision of welfare benefits. Schemes involving government activity in the area of welfare are many and various. They may have different objectives, even where they are promoting the same values.

Such schemes fall into three categories which it is important to distinguish. The first are welfare schemes which aim to return people to the productive economy who for one reason or another have fallen out of it, but who possess or can acquire the skills and capacities to become active, self-reliant participants in the market economy. These are claims, for example, to unemployment benefits, to retraining schemes, to remedial education and so forth. These are welfare benefits whose aim is to promote the autonomy of members of underclass groups by returning them to and reintegrating them into the market economy. It is a point of cardinal importance that *these* welfare benefits always carry with them obligations—to engage in workfare, or to accept reasonable employment once re-skilled, for example. In Britain, policy on unemployment is almost the worst imaginable, with stagnant pools of the long-term unemployed living by eking out their low benefits, without having in most cases any real prospect of genuine reskilling. Policy-makers in Britain could with profit study labour policy in Sweden, where very generous assistance in reskilling is given but has attached to it an obligation to accept employment in the areas for which the person has been retrained. One consequence of this—one neglected by American and British neo-liberal and neo-conservative theorists, who argue that welfare institutions always generate dependency—is that Sweden (whatever its other problems may be and whatever may have caused the political changes of late 1991) has no underclass, or only a very small one, of the multi-generationally unemployed.

In our society, having a job is for most people a basic need, since for most people involuntary long-term unemployment deals a severe blow to self-esteem. A welfare entitlement to reskilling, whenever this is feasible, together with the complimentary obligations, is for this reason one element in the matrix of welfare policies that promote autonomy. Among us, literacy and numeracy are necessary conditions of almost any kind of autonomous life, so that access to education is also a welfare right. We have here an instance of the second class of welfare benefit, those designed to prepare people for the status of autonomous individuals in a liberal civil society. How this welfare benefit to education is to be embodied is a matter for reasonable debate. I have elsewhere speculated in Millian terms[73] that a privatised schooling system, with targeted vouchers and merit bursaries for the needy, might be the best system to this end, but in the present context it is the principle of education as a valid welfare claim rather than the institutional means for guaranteeing it (which will greatly vary according to circumstances) that is most important to establish.

What of health care? In which category of welfare benefit does it fall? Here we need to distinguish among different categories of health care, and the various means whereby it might be provided. In respect of catastrophic and chronic serious illness, and of most forms of disability, especially in its more severe forms, we have a clearly distinct third form of welfare benefit, that (unlike the first) does not carry with it concomitant obligations. When their capital is exhausted, or their incomes are low, people falling into this category have a welfare claim to whatever services are needed to enable them to lead a life that is as autonomous, as dignified and as meaningful as that of able-bodied persons, in so far as this is achievable. Incentive considerations are largely irrelevant here. Such persons possess welfare claims with no corresponding duties. Policy in this area has been particularly poor in Britain, and may well get even worse. As I have elsewhere argued, a voucher-based scheme for community care[74] seems particularly appropriate in that it combines a guarantee of public provision with individual choice of its forms made in competitive free markets. This is a point to which I shall return later in general terms.

It is here that Raz's observations on the satiability of most basic needs are relevant. Raz illuminates a fundamental property of basic needs, as distinct from wants or preferences, when he notes that, most of them, in principle, are capable of complete satiation. The needs of the disabled, or of the illiterate, though sometimes perhaps expensive to meet, can be met completely, that is to say, to the point at which they can lead reasonably autonomous lives. The crucial conceptual distinction is made by Raz[75] when he notes that happiness is a satiable value, whereas pleasure is not. A person with a happy life need have no reason to seek to improve his life, whereas someone devoted to pleasure always has reason to seek more pleasure. Most basic needs have the property of satiability, which means that, once they are met, the content of the welfare claim which guarantees their satisfaction is exhausted.

Medical care generates peculiarly difficult problems, not only for the thesis advocated here, but for *all* views in that by no means all medical needs are fully satiable. Whereas those of the disabled are usually fully satiable, those connected with the process of aging, or with illnesses that are terminal but which can (with an ever worsening quality of life) be indefinitely staved-off, sometimes are not. The problem of basic needs that are non-satiable is a hard one for any theory, or, at least, for any theory that is unprepared to consider the legitimacy of euthanasia. This is not a problem on which I can hope to say anything useful in this context, though I am sure that Dutch policy on euthanasia merits careful study, as does the admirable American legal innovation, the Living Will (which mandates withdrawal of life-support systems under certain conditions).

Against the thesis that welfare benefits are valid claims to the satisfaction of basic needs, it will doubtless be objected that the scope and content of any basic need is disputable and perhaps arbitrary. More subtly, it may be objected[76] that basic needs may be incommensurable, in that satisfying them yields no overall measure of need satisfaction. In response to these objections, it must be accepted that at least those basic needs not having to do with biological survival will have a significant cultural or conventional dimension. The basic needs of a Kalahari bushman will not be the same as those of a young urban professional. It is hard to see, however, how this evident variability in the content of basic needs across cultures and societies renders them altogether subjective. In any particular society, reasoned public discourse can occur as to the content of basic needs, which invokes the shared norms and common life of the society. Such discourse will never achieve the precise objectivity of the natural sciences, but that will be an objection to it only for those (and there are many) who have forgotten (or never known) Aristotle's wise dictum that we should only expect in any subject the kind and degree of precision of which it is capable.

The objection that the scope and content of basic needs is disputable, and the implication that the stability of basic needs is therefore delusive, presupposes that the indeterminacies in the account of basic needs are remedied, or avoided, in other theories. It is difficult to see what sustains this illusion. The indeterminacy that afflicts discourse about basic needs is merely an instance of the pervasive indeterminacy that haunts moral and political discourse. It is not a defect of the theory, but rather a fact of life. The favourite policy measures of latter-day classical liberals—the negative income tax and voucher schemes, for example—themselves confront precisely the same indeterminacies. What should be the size of a school voucher, and how (and by whom) is this to be determined? What level of income is to be specified as the minimum in a negative income tax scheme, and how can such a specification avoid invoking contestable value-judgements about the level of subsistence? Or, to turn to the functions of the so-called minimum state, to what level of police protection are citizens entitled, and by what formula is this to be decided? It is evident that classical liberal principles and proposals are beset by all of the indeterminacies that afflict my own. This is a point not without practical significance, as I shall show in the last chapter of this paper, when I come to consider the case of a government that sought to implement the ideas sketched here about an enabling welfare state.

The deeper objection concerns the commensurability of basic needs. Among medical needs, can the preservation of life be ranked against the alleviation of pain? And how are medical needs to be weighed against educational or intellectual needs? It would seem that such judgments could be made, if at all, only by invoking a thick and comprehensive conception of the good life about which there is, among us, no consensus. Distribution according to basic needs would then be arbitrary, in that it would impose on all a conception of the good life that was only one of several, possibly incommensurable conceptions harboured in our society. What can be said against this claim? An answer can be found, I believe, in the fact that the content of a basic need is subject to partial self-definition by the agent. A person may have basic medical needs which require residence in a nursing home, but the detailed mixture of goods and services may again be determined by the person himself. Equally, a person may have a basic need for literacy, but the form in which this is satisfied—the mode of teaching and learning—may be decided by the person himself. This is especially so, if the guarantee of the basic need comes in the form of a voucher which the person may spend on a range of services. Vouchers are in this sense a species of welfare benefit that is akin to a positive right.

Nor is the incommensurability of basic needs an obstacle to their satiability. For, as Raz has observed, 'satiability does not mean that there is a point which is reached by all who get to the point of satiation (in the alleviation of hunger, the satisfaction of needs, or in happiness, etc.) such that they are all at precisely the same level in the relevant respect. All it implies is that there is no possibility of improving the positions they reached. That condition is satisfied by complete incommensurability of happiness once a certain level of it is reached'.[77] If we allow, as in voucher schemes, a partial self-definition of basic needs, then these may be satiated, even if the needs concerned are not commensurable. Difficulties arise, so far as I can see, only in areas of policy where basic needs are not satiable, or where there is radical resource-scarcity in respect of satiable basic needs. In these areas, voucher schemes may be neither appropriate nor workable. This illustrates a central aspect of my argument—that all welfare policies and institutions, like all other policies and institutions, have costs, hazards and other imperfections. For this reason, no single measure can conceivably be adequate to our concerns, and all will have side-effects that are regrettable.

It is worth saying something as to the institutional and policy framework of an enabling welfare state, with particular reference to issues of universality *versus* selectivity, and entitlement *versus* discretion in welfare benefits. Let us take, first, the issue of universality *versus* targeting. It is reasonable to target welfare benefits when, but only when, this does not generate perverse incentive structures and impose heavy informational and administrative costs on welfare institutions. These conditions are rarely met except in the area of benefits for the disabled and long term sick, where incomes and capital holdings are fairly easily assessed, and incentive considerations are insignificant. Elsewhere, there are massive incentive and epistemic objections to targeting, and good arguments for universal provision. Targeting policies in welfare face grave epistemic problems in assessing needs that are often variable, and whose measurement is disputable. In respect of the favoured neo-liberal measure of the negative income tax, how would it cope with the fluctuating incomes of seasonal and part-time workers? What would be the unit of assessment—individual or household? If household, how could that be defined? In addition to massive epistemic difficulties, the negative income tax, with its usual marginal tax rate of around 70 per cent, would generate huge disincentives and a deep poverty trap. It is hard to see why this absurd measure (with its inevitable consequence of a further large socialisation of income) has gained the support of so many neo-liberals.

Because of the epistemic and incentive difficulties of targeting, there is a strong case for universal provision where, as in the unreformed National Health Service (with all its imperfections), costs can be maintained at comparatively reasonable levels and a decent basic level of treatment provided in most areas of need. It is a signal advantage of universal provision that, unlike targeting schemes, it does not skew incentives perversely so as to create poverty traps, make unreasonable demands on the knowledge possessed by providers, or generate vast administrative apparatuses. It is therefore preferable to targeting in such areas as the NHS and, as has already been suggested here, the basic state pension. This is not to say that means-testing is never appropriate, since policy areas have been noted where it may well be; only that in many policy areas the costs of selectivity far outweigh the benefits.

Consider next the issue of discretion *versus* entitlement in welfare benefits. Neo-liberals have shown a fondness for discretion in welfare policy that is strange, given their concern for the limitation of power over the lives of individuals.

The model of discretionary allocation by governmental authority (as practised in Switzerland, for example) should be objectionable to liberals for several reasons. It concentrates power over the lives of individuals, often vulnerable or defenceless individuals, to a wholly objectionable extent. Because the authority exercised is discretionary, it cannot conform to any ideal of the rule of law, which in other areas liberals cherish. In practice, welfare benefits will be allocated at the discretion of welfare professionals whose decisions will often (if experience is any guide) be animated by questionable orthodoxies and ephemeral fads. And, because in practice the discretionary authority is bound to be subject to budgetary constraints, the integrity of that authority as the guardian of the recipients' interests and needs will inevitably be compromised. This is a major defect of the Griffith Report on community care, which proposes replacement of the present system's voucher arrangement by bureaucratic assessment of individual needs, and of current reform proposals for the NHS which reinforce discretionary allocation of medical resources while at the same time compromising the clinical freedom of doctors. Finally, liberals who oppose entrenched welfare entitlements may care to recall that they were also rejected by socialists, such as the Webbs, apparently because they believed that they accorded to individuals an undue freedom of choice.

None of this is to say that discretionary allocation of welfare benefits may not sometimes be desirable, or else inevitable—as, perhaps, in the case of the Social Fund in Britain. Over a large area of benefits, however, there is a strong case for their entrenchment as entitlements, given the uncertainty and arbitrariness that go with discretionary allocation. In many cases, voucher schemes should be expanded or instituted, being themselves (as has already been observed) entrenched welfare entitlements. Critics of welfare entitlements may, then, reasonably be asked why they support species of them (such as voucher schemes) and yet resist the extension of such schemes into other areas of welfare policy.

A genuinely liberal approach to welfare policy will, accordingly, favour an enabling welfare state, featuring universality and entitlement in many areas of provision. It will however be a pluralist institution, containing policies and practices of targeting and discretionary allocation, where these seem the only appropriate measures. It will not attempt the impossible (and, in my view, undesirable) task of imposing any pattern of distribution on society, a task ruled out by the same epistemic and incentive arguments that defeat central planning. It will rely, so far as is feasible, on the institutions and informal life of civil society, where local knowledge can be best deployed. In its own operations, the enabling welfare state will see to it that benefits such as workfare, confer obligations, where they can reasonably be imposed; that they be means-tested, where (as in the context of chronic illness) incentive considerations are insignificant; and it will seek to devolve welfare functions to the lowest level of government, thus observing the principle of subsidiarity while acknowledging the necessity of central governmental funding. Where feasible and cost-effective it will separate governmental funding from governmental provision, using vouchers and other devices to give state support to market provision of welfare services. It will not, however, suppose that privatisation and marketisation are the answers to all problems in welfare policy.

The enabling welfare state here advocated differs from others in that its ethical foundation is not in ideas of justice or distribution, still less in ideas of fundamental rights, but rather in the values of autonomy and enablement that ground market institutions. The individuals who are enabled to act autonomously by market institutions and by the institutions of an enabling welfare state will enjoy rich autonomy only if there are forms of common life, rich in choice-worthy options, available to them. It is these forms of community that the social market economy aims to nurture and protect.

7

The Social Market Economy: An Outline

According to the perspective which animates this paper, there is an essential indeterminacy about which goods are to be produced in markets. There is no general, universal principle that can tell us which goods are best provided by markets, by voluntary associations, by the institutions of an enabling welfare state, by collective political decision-making or by the application of a rule or the invocation of an entitlement. Time, place and circumstance have always a major contribution to make to our deliberations on these matters. In any particular historical context, however, there are considerations or maxims which assist us in our detailed, circumstantial reasonings as to which goods are best supplied by markets and which by other institutions. Elsewhere[78], I have stated a few of these maxims, including the central one that, aside from the core state activities of national defense and law and order, the vast majority of economic goods are in a modern state such as Britain most appropriately supplied in free markets (supplemented, where necessary, by voucher and other schemes for the provision of purchasing power to those otherwise without income or resources). This maxim is further supported by the upshot of the argument earlier in this paper, which is that no modern state can in the end avoid the bulk of economic activities being conducted within the institutions of a free market economy. This is so, both for practical (epistemic and incentive) reasons and for ethical reasons having to do with the promotion of individual autonomy. Another way of stating this result is to say that it is only through the institutions of a liberal civil society—in which contractual freedom, personal liberty and private property are protected under a rule of law—that a modern civilisation can reproduce itself. I have passed over here the important area of those individual liberties that are exercised in economic and commercial life, not because they are unimportant, but because others have shown their indispensable role in a liberal civil society, and I have elsewhere myself argued to that effect.[79] It is maintained here that market institutions are an aspect of individual freedom, conceived as autonomy, that is indivisible from other dimensions of autonomy, such as those protected by freedoms of conscience, expression and so on. This is a result of the argument that will be taken as given in the subsequent discussion, and which underpins the later discussion of the outlines of a social market economy in Britain.

My topic here is that of the limits of market institutions—the question of the areas in which there is market failure, or in which market provision is inappropriate for other reasons, or requires supplementation. It may be worth repeating here that the shape of market institutions is not something that can be known *a priori*, or which can be derived from any theory—say, a theory of rights. On the view developed here—a view which I owe to the Freiburg School of social market theorists—market institutions are social constructions, artifacts which we may not have designed, and which are for us historical inheritances, but which we may properly alter and reform so that they better contribute to human well-being. There is not, in other words, *an ideal market*, a condition of pure *laissez-faire*, to which real markets approximate; there are only the varied institutions that make up markets in all their diversity. Like every other human institution, the market is imperfect (and imperfectible); and there is no single, unique set of market institutions that is everywhere and always appropriate. The spirit in which we approach market institutions ought, perhaps, to be that of Popper's piecemeal social engineer,[80] who seeks to improve institutions bit by bit, without the dubious assistance of any model of perfection. If we approach markets in this spirit, we will find that they often need to be supplemented or informed by government action if they are to achieve their ends and make their contribution to human well-being.

The most obvious area in which the limits of market institutions are revealed is that of *public goods*—goods which, because they are not partitionable or excludable, must be supplied to all or none. It is not such goods—goods such as clean air, say—that I will address here. Many other writers have said all that can be usefully said on the subject, including the wise observation that the dangers of market failure must always be weighed against the hazards of government failure. I shall instead focus upon another kind of public good; those *inherently* public goods (in Raz's terms[81]) that are associated with a public culture in which autonomous individuals have a rich array of options and amenities to choose from. In part, to be sure, this latter species of public good overlaps with the former. A clean city or natural environment may be a public good in both senses. The sense with which I am here concerned, however, is that in which a city, say, that is not only clean, but also safe, pleasing to the senses and contains a good variety of cultural amenities, forms the public space in which individuals may make autonomous choices among valuable options. The insight that is being exploited here (which I owe to Raz's work) is that autonomy, if it is to be meaningful and valuable, requires not only capacities for choice on the part of the individual, but also a span of worthwhile options in his cultural environment. In the absence of this, autonomy wanes, and the lives of individuals become the poorer, however many choices they make. Autonomy is not worth much, if it is exercised in a Hobbesian state of nature.

The area of policy identified by this concern is primarily that of *environmental policy*, both in respect of the natural and the humanly constructed environment. In both cases, a rich environment conducive to valuable autonomy can be promoted by market institutions, by road pricing in cities as an antidote to traffic congestion, and by an appropriate tax regime for polluters and the creation or refinement of property rights in natural spaces. It is silly, nonetheless, to suppose that market institutions alone can protect the integrity of the environment. No market solution exists, so far as we know, for the greenhouse effect. Further, providing or renewing a decent urban environment requires private *and* public investment in infrastructure. A liberal state committed to assuring the public space in which autonomous individuals make their choices cannot be indifferent to the physical and social environment. In that regard, the model from which we have most to learn is that of Austria, Germany and Scandinavia, in which the social market economy provides the resources whereby a graceful and elegant urban environment is maintained. It is to the countries of continental Europe, again, rather than to the United States, whose history and geography may make other policies more appropriate, that we should look for a model for *transport policy* in which otherwise excessive reliance on the private automobile is diminished and public transport systems encouraged, where necessary by subsidy.

It is in regard to the cultural environment in which autonomous choices must be made that a liberal state has its most controversial responsibilities. A cultural environment in which family breakdown is commonplace, in which the arts and the sciences are neglected and in which the level of public taste is vulgar, is an impoverished one in which few options will be choice-worthy. For the most part, of course, we must rely on the autonomous intermediary institutions of civil society to prevent this impoverishment, and there is much that can be done by way of tax deductibility in these areas whereby the vitality of civil society can be maintained and enhanced. This is *not* to say that Britain, or any other modern state, can sensibly do without an *arts policy* which encourages and supports cultural activities (such as opera) which could not otherwise be sustained. The libertarian objection that such subsidy is regressive in its incidence on the population is not a sensible one, since the goal of such support is not distributional. Its justification is what is termed in recent philosophy *perfectionist*[82]—it aims to support forms of activity that are intrinsically valuable, whosoever consumes or enjoys them. Nor is the argument that public support for the arts depends on an arbitrary judgment about the value of the activity one which has any force. It has force, if at all, only if we adopt a blank value-scepticism in which we view judgements of the value of pigeon-fancying or pornography against the plays of Shakespeare or the novels of Dostoevsky, say, as entirely subjective, reflecting or expressing only the personal preference of the judge. Such a perspective, containing only preferences, may seem a natural one for economists, but it is not one a policy-maker has any good reason to accept.

In practical policy terms, the implication of the argument that a society without a flourishing artistic life and a higher culture in which art objects have a status other than commodities is an impoverished one would be, in the area of the deregulation of television, for example, the proposal for an Arts Council of the Air—one advanced by distinguished classical liberals such as Brittan and Peacock.[83] An analogous argument can be made for *science policy*, whose aim should be to encourage and support pure research, and to prevent science being reduced to an entirely utilitarian activity conducted in a context of chronic resource-scarcity. In both areas, the underlying argument is that the activity, art or science, is itself *an intrinsic good*, whose value is not reducible to the satisfaction of personal preferences. Moreover, it is an intrinsic good which opens up for the autonomous chooser options in the common culture without which he, like it, would be the poorer, and which thereby enhance his autonomy. In respect of the cultural environment, there is a strong case to be made that institutions such as the BBC should not be undermined in a circumstance in which alternative institutions, at least as efficacious in maintaining cultural standards, have yet to prove themselves.

Autonomous choosers cannot flourish in an environment of anomic individuals, lacking in the capacities necessary for responsibility and for intrinsically valuable relationships such as those of romantic love and friendship. An autonomous chooser surrounded by wantons[84]—by persons without ethical standards, long-term projects or deep attachments—will lead an empty life, however resourceful he may otherwise be. A liberal state therefore has the vital responsibility of tending and sheltering the institutional matrix of responsible choosers, the family. It cannot for that reason shirk the formulation of a *family policy*. In this, though it ought to eschew the spurious liberal ideal of neutrality with regard to all forms of family life, it is bound to respect the legitimate variety of forms of family life we find among us. In other words, though policy should aim to discourage forms of family life, such as that of single-parenthood where it is demonstrably injurious to children, it cannot engage in projects of social engineering aiming to revive a vanished form of traditional family life. Appropriate policies in this area might include tax deductibility or subsidies for child care at work, an increase of child benefits for the under-fives and compelling absent fathers to provide for their offspring at the levels determined by the courts.[85] Whatever the detailed mix of measures, a liberal government cannot responsibly avoid developing a policy on the family.

This is only one instance of a more general point, that a liberal regime concerned to promote the autonomy of its subjects cannot avoid concerning itself with the social forms in which autonomy is exercised. The worth, perhaps the very existence, of autonomous choices depends on the existence of these social forms. As Raz has again put it:

> ...individuals inevitably derive the goals by which they constitute their lives from the stock of social forms available to them, and the feasible variations on it... By being teachers, production workers, drivers, public servants, loyal friends and family people, loyal to their communities, nature-lovers and so on they will be pursuing their own goals, enhancing their own well-being, and also serving their communities, and generally living in a morally worthy way.[86]

In general, valuable autonomy presupposes a stock of roles, statuses, institutions and social forms, a structure of intermediary institutions embodied in a common culture, from which individuals derive worthwhile options. A liberal government has a positive responsibility to tend and nurture these intermediary institutions, and ought never to make policy on the model of the atomistic individual related to others only by a variety of contractual agreements.

What are the responsibilities of government in respect of the market economy itself? By far the most important is that of the provision of a stable currency—an objective on which all recent British governments have defaulted. It is naive in the extreme to suppose that this can be achieved while *monetary policy* remains politicised. A market solution, such as the Hayekian[87] proposal for competing currencies, may be defensible, but is not at present in the realm of the politically possible, and might not provide an antidote to inflation until that had reached unacceptable levels. In all likelihood, the institutional framework best suited to monetary stability is not that of the market, still less that of the political sphere in which democratic governments will inevitably debase the currency in the futile attempt to bring into an advantageous alignment the electoral and the economic cycles. The most promising framework is that of a regime of rules, whether as embodied in an independent central bank (as in New Zealand) or in a regime of fixed exchange rates, as advocated by the earlier Hayek. The paramount dangers to stable money in our times are those of democratic political competition and of monetary nationalism. For this reason the custody of a sound currency is in contemporary circumstances not something that can safely be left to national governments, or to the devices of markets that governments will unavoidably manipulate. Instead, the provision of a sound currency can only be solved by a regime of rules that constrains or prevents monetary debasement by government. In the British case, ERM membership with all its costs and imperfections, has at least proved a significant constraint on currency debasement by government. However, ERM membership, because of its distortive effects on the British economy, and the difficulty, perhaps, for epistemic reasons, the impossibility of determining the 'right' rate of the pound within it, is a poor substitute for sound domestic monetary policy. In the British case, the best prospects for stable money lie in the establishment of a truly independent bank, modelled on the New Zealand example, in which its policies are guided by rules, rather than on the American model of the Federal Reserve Bank, whose discretionary authority allows it to pursue (as at present) devaluationist and inflationary policies. If in Britain we possessed a central bank that was genuinely independent of government in its policies, ERM membership would be at best unnecessary or, more likely, undesirable.

Aside from depoliticising monetary policy, one of the most important tasks of a liberal state is a negative one—that of refraining from developing an industrial strategy. Such a policy—a policy of picking winners, and supporting them by tariff or subsidy—is one of the inheritances of corporatism in Britain, and has a dismal record of failure. In this connection, we have much to learn from Germany and Japan, in which (contrary to popular opinion) the effect of government superintendence of the economy has been to promote intense internal competition. The epistemic argument against socialism, though it is certainly not a conclusive argument against *all* forms of government intervention in the economy, is certainly a powerful one against an industrial policy that aims to guide the economy as a whole. In this respect, nothing could be more pernicious than the idiom of *UK plc*, with its insidious echoes of a bankrupt corporatism.

This is *not* to endorse *laissez-faire* (itself probably an historical illusion), nor to say that there should be a 'hands-off' policy of government in all areas of the economy. A *regional policy* of tax reductions, enterprise zones and so forth is plainly arguable. A *labour policy*, preferably on Swedish lines, has already been mentioned as an element in the enabling welfare state aiming to return to autonomy and productivity those who have fallen out of (or never been in) the market economy. Without returning to the corporatist illusion of incomes policies, it is not clear that a *wage policy* cannot be formulated by government which assists wage bargaining in the market environment. And it is hard to see how any modern state can eschew the formulation of an *energy policy*, itself an integral part of policy toward the environment.

It has not been the aim here to discuss exhaustively all those governmental activities which seek to supplement market provision of goods and services. I have not discussed *tax policy*, save in passing, nor have I said much (except in passing) about *education policy* or *social policy*, since, crucially important as they are, they are beyond my brief here. The philosophical thesis of this paper is that completeness or determinacy in regard to a specification of the proper spheres of government, market and voluntary association is in any case an impossibility, a figment spawned by the hubris of theory. The aim here has been the humbler one of arguing that this ineradicable indeterminacy need not inhibit reasoned circumstantial discourse and debate about the roles of market, voluntary association and government in a modern state such as ours. The functions I have ascribed to government, and the range of policies that I have argued come under its responsibility, are far larger than anything acceptable to a libertarian or a classical liberal perspective, yet considerably smaller than those required by a socialist or an egalitarian social-democratic perspective. It has in fact been one of the postulates of my argument that no modern state will in fact retreat to the sphere of minimum government, any more than any modern state will succeed in generating an egalitarian community. Brute historical facts, such as mass democracy and cultural pluralism, together with the imperatives of the market economy itself, render these visions utopian fantasies (or, as I would view them, dystopian nightmares). But I have also tried to exhibit the ethical and philosophical reasons why these ideals have no claim on morality or on our reason.

On the positive side, my argument has been that market competition is not a natural feature of human behaviour, but an institutional artifact, a process occurring within or generated by a definite (though variable across time and space) matrix of laws and policies. It was, in fact, one of the central insights of the German social market model which animates much of my argument that the free market requires more than non-intervention by government to preserve competition—it requires a *competition policy*, as recognised in the Dusseldorf Principles enunciated by the Christian Democrats in 1949, which stipulated 'competition guaranteed by control of monopoly'. The recognition that governmental intervention may be a necessary precondition of market competition is one of the essential features of the social market economy model.

What, in outline, are the other constitutive features of the social market economy? It may be worth pausing here, if only briefly, to rebut the standard objections, made by classical or fundamentalist liberals, to the very expression. Often, it is maintained that the expression is tautologous, since markets are themselves social institutions, presupposing and generating a host of social relationships, not all of which are economic in the narrow sense. Alternatively, though incompatibly, it is often held that the expression is oxymoronic, in that markets do not exist to serve any social or collective end, but simply to satisfy the disparate purposes of individuals. Or, lastly, it is commonly alleged that the expression has no clear meaning at all.

These common objections are mentioned, not because they have any force, but so as to explain the central tenets of the social market economy, as it is theorized in the Freiburg School, and as it might be realised in the specific context of contemporary Britain. One of the key ideas has already been stated in the argument thus far—that the market is not a natural social phenomenon, but instead a creature of law and government. A second idea is that the market is not free-standing or self-justifying, but part of a larger nexus of institutions, sharing with them a justification in terms of the contribution it makes to human well-being. A third idea is that the market lacks ethical and political legitimacy unless it is supplemented or complemented by other institutions that temper its excesses and correct its failures. Market institutions will lack legitimacy, if market exchanges occur in filthy or unsafe environments, if there is not a rich infrastructure of public amenities that undergirds them, or if there exists an underclass that is denied access to them. The theory of the social market economy, at its core, is that market institutions are always embedded in other social and political institutions, which both shape them and legitimate them.

The central ideas of the *Soziale Markwirtschaft* have been characterised by Hutchinson as Smithian in mode:

> This 'Smithian' mode, starting from a realistic view of man and his psychology, and recognizing the all-pervasiveness of ignorance in human affairs, gives as important a place in its objectives to freedom and the rule of law as it does to the attainment of some ideal, optimal economic efficiency. The ideal behind the launching of the Social-Market Economy, coming down, as they did, in part from the Historical School, followed this 'Smithian' mode. For example, Walter Eucken laid great emphasis on the 'interdependence between the economic order and all other forms of order (i.e. legal, social and political)'... Eucken condemned the policy of *laissez-faire* as incompatible with the maintenance of a legal order based on the idea of a *Rechtstaat*, because such a policy conceded too much power to monopolies and partial monopolies.[88]

It had been Eucken, of course, who in his seminal 1948 article, 'On the Theory of the Centrally Administered Economy: an Analysis of the German Experiment', had shown not only the inevitable inefficiency, but also the incompatibility with individual freedom and the rule of law, of central planning in the German case. It was these ideas which animated the bold experiment in deregulation, inaugurated by Erhard against the wishes of the Allied Occupying Powers, which began the German economic miracle. It is these ideas—the ideas of *Ordoliberalismus* and the Freiburg School—that most merit study in Britain at present. They do so, in the first place, because the German case is the *only* one, so far, in which the role of government in the economy and in society has been radically, and seemingly irreversibly, reduced. As Hutchinson observes:

> ...so persistent, and seemingly ineluctable, has been the extension of the role of government in so many economically advanced, democratic countries, that it is difficult to cite any case from such countries where a significant rolling back of the interventionist tide has been achieved, *except after major wars*. Even there, the role of government in the economy has usually only been reduced as compared with the all-pervasive central regulation of wartime, and not nearly pushed back to the previous peacetime level.
>
> To these generalisations the Social Market Economy of the German Federal Republic has presided the outstanding among leading Western democratic countries.[89]

Published in 1981, Hutchinson's statement needs no revision a decade later, when the delusive revolutions of Thatcher and Reagan have left government larger that ever before in peacetime in their respective countries. There is a second reason why these ideas—ideas carried on by such thinkers as Gottfried Lutz, and influencing others such as Alfred Müller-Armack—should be studied in Britain. This is that the social-market theorists of a free economic order, or *Ordnung*, recognised (as the neo-liberal architects of the failed Thatcher and Reagan revolutions did not) that free-market institutions, if they were to be enduring and legitimate, had to be embedded in broader, social and political institutions, which shaped and constrained them. As Hutchinson puts it:

> The other (Smithian or social-market) kind of case for the competitive market economy is (by contrast with the neoclassical, Ricardian case) formulated in much broader terms, comprehending the political and social order, and especially the legal foundations and framework of the economic order.[90]

And Hutchinson remarked of Eucken that

> 'the launching of the Social-Market Economy was and had to be an explicitly "constructivist" act'.

As Eucken put it:

> 'The economic system has to be consciously shaped'.[91]

Market institutions, then, although they always comprehend an inheritance of evolved conventions and practices, are always open to reform or redesign, and such modifications are and should be part of a deliberate policy which recognises and takes into account the embeddedness of market institutions in other, legal, social and political institutions.

Such institutions will have no unique structure, but will vary in their shape and content from time to time and place to place. It is not here being proposed that the German model, in its theory or its practice, should (or could) be simply transplanted to Britain. The proposal is that market institutions in Britain, and perhaps other similar modern states, require for their legitimacy a variety of governmental policies and institutions, including the institution of an enabling welfare state. This is to say that the structure, content and legitimacy of market institutions is guaranteed by the legal and social intervention of an active government. (It is not claimed that an enabling welfare state, as such, was a part of the German social market economy; only that, in Britain today, it best complements market institutions, and so captures the spirit of the social market economy.)[92] Freeing up the market, and reducing the invasive state, require accordingly a positive, and not only a negative agenda of governmental policy. This is affirmed against the background of a prior affirmation—that government should enter only where private provision and voluntary association are demonstrably inadequate. In other words, as has already been noted, *the principle of subsidiarity*—the principle that government ought not to usurp functions that can be well discharged by intermediary institutions—ought to be observed throughout policy.

It may nevertheless be reasonably asked how large will be the kind of state mandated by my theorising. In part, the answer is that the legitimate concern ought to be with *what* the state properly does, *not* with its overall magnitude. After all, a state could have only a few functions, most of them undesirable and yet pre-empt most of society's resources so as to discharge them.

Again, there will presumably be few who would opt for a state that pre-empted a quarter of society's resources but wasted most of them, over a state that controlled slightly more but spent them judiciously in the service of agreed and desirable objectives. It cannot, then, sensibly be the sheer size of a state, independently of any other criterion, that determines its legitimacy.

Nor is the demand that the state that is justified by the theory I have advanced be determinate in its size at all a sensible one. It is radically flawed at both philosophical and empirical levels. It expresses the superstition, cherished by classical or fundamentalist liberals, that there is a talismanic formula, an infallible theory or unfailing legal or constitutional device, that can determine, presumably forever, the proper scope and functions of the state. In its most primitive form, this is the theory of the minimum state, with all its incoherencies. Its inadequacies are patent. Do the minimum functions of government include the provision of a sound currency, or not? If they are restricted to national defence and law and order, how is the size of those functions to be determined, and how are they to be financed? If minimal government is to encompass voucher schemes or negative income tax schemes, how is the size of those to be decided and their costs defrayed? These are questions to which classical liberal theory gives no determinate answers, if only because there are none to be given. The indeterminacy they fail to overcome is not a defect of any theory, including that developed in this paper; it is merely a truth about the world.

The objection that the state emerging from the theory defended here is indeterminate in its size or cost is similarly absurd at the level of practice. It is true that the public choice process theorized in the economic theories of bureaucracy and democracy could have the perverse effect of inflating an enabling welfare state, say, beyond the functions envisaged here. This danger is inherent in every other governmental institution and policy. It would occur in the minimum state, as will be recognised by anyone with any knowledge of the realities of military procurement in the United States and elsewhere. It would occur, and occur on a stupendous level, if the disastrous neo-liberal panacea of the negative income-tax were instituted: it would at once be bid up by the vote motive to the level of tolerance of consequent taxation, or beyond. It would manifestly be the case in respect of such other neo-liberal measures as voucher schemes: since their size and cost would undoubtedly be inflated by the pressures of political competition, they have (in *that* respect) no advantage whatever over other forms of governmental provision. The same is true of tax credits, for which there would in practice be an undignified political auction. Note, in passing, that public choice theory predicts expansionist tendencies in governmental services, even in the absence of the democratic vote motive, in virtue of bureaucratic rent-seeking. Partly for this reason, the knee-jerk classical liberal response to the objections here advanced—that such measures be governed by constitutional rules or analogous devices—is (perhaps incorrigibly) naive. The example of balanced budget rules, which have everywhere been circumvented and honoured in the breach, illustrates the futility of such devices. The truth is that, aside from the constant vigilance of a citizenry steeped in a culture of liberty, there is no remedy for the expansionist tendencies inherent in all forms of government activity. This is as true for the so-called minimum state, and for the favoured measures of neo-liberalism, as it is for any other. Is this simple truth in fact so subtle as to elude the understanding of latter-day classical liberals? It is, after all, only an instance of the imperfect-ibility of all human institutions—itself an exceedingly ancient truth.

At the same time, the concern that an invasive state will stifle the autonomy of civil society is a compelling one that must be addressed. The argument of this paper is that reductions in government expenditure ought to be qualitative, not quantitat-ive, across-the-board cuts. A state that sheltered a liberal civil society, in which the freedoms of the market economy were tempered by the institution of an enabling welfare state and supplemented by a variety of other institutions and measures, need not be a large state. It would likely be much smaller than most existing democratic states.

The size and invasiveness of the state can be reduced significantly, in ways compatible with the measures advocated here, principally because much current government expenditure consists in a wasteful system of cross-subsidies to the middle classes. In Britain, for example, state expenditure on the so-called underclass is probably only about one-sixth of total expenditure on welfare as a whole. (The situation is likely little different in the United States.) It is therefore a travesty to represent the existing British welfare state, either as a system of organised altruism for the benefit of the poor and needy, as socialists sometimes do, or a vast system of unjust transfers from the majority, as many classical liberals and conservatives sometimes do. In harsh reality, the income transfers of the welfare state, especially when taken in conjunction with the tax regime, are in substantial part transfers from the rich and the poor minorities to the middle-class majority. (In Britain, there may be good reason to retain universal provision in some areas, such as the NHS, where there are perverse transfers, but where the costs of targeting are excessive. This may not be so in other countries, such as New Zealand, where the health care delivery system to be reformed has long contained charges.) With the exception of a few of its programmes, the British welfare state is a middle-class racket without ethical justification or standing, and which (because of its vast transaction costs and wastefulness) does not in the end benefit even the middle classes.

The size and cost of a welfare state instituting a system of welfare rights could well be far less than that of the current welfare state, if (like present crypto-voucher schemes in community care) welfare benefits were targeted, if many welfare benefits conferred obligations on their recipients, and if the tax system provided better incentives for self-provision. A system of proportional taxation, in which redistributions were made transparently from the affluent majority to the needy minorities, might make the advantages of a welfare state streamlined to serve the genuinely needy clearer to all. It is a cardinal point of the present argument that, whereas much welfare spending in Britain is wasteful and ineffective, an enabling welfare state ought to aim for a far more complete satisfaction of the basic needs of the unfortunate than is presently achieved.

In the British case, if neo-liberal, supply-side arguments about tax revenue rising as marginal rates are lowered have any substance, better provision could be made for the beneficiaries of an enabling welfare state at the lower income tax rate of 20 per cent, perhaps, levied proportionally.

It is hard, but perhaps not altogether impossible, to see how these harsh realities could be reformed, given the facts of political competition in mass democracy. They could be so reformed, only if the middle classes could be persuaded that a smaller state, in which under a lower tax regime they were free to provide most services privately for themselves, was more in their interests than the current ruleless and wasteful *melange* of arrangements. That is a demanding political task for any party. Though daunting, we should not allow excessive cynicism about democratic political life in Britain to convince us of the impossibility of such a reform. There is a real danger that the Public Choice model of the economics of politics (which has illuminated much—especially in the work of James Buchanan—that is vitally important for our understanding of the processes of political competition) could blind us to the shared norms that pervade political life—in Britain at any rate—and which constrain policies founded solely on a calculation of their economic costs and benefits to voters. The fiasco of the so-called community charge, which offended the sense of fairness even of many who were gainers from it, has a lesson to teach (for those who can learn from it) about the limitations of a purely economic analysis of political life, and the dangers of policies based on such a model. More positively, the manifest limitations of the Public Choice model in its application to British political life suggest that the moral appeal of the sort of society resulting from the reforms suggested may have a political resonance, even for those who might initially lose from them, that should not be dogmatically discounted. This is the challenge that must be addressed by any serious liberal reform of current arrangements.

Unless it is confronted, there is no real prospect of reforming present arrangements so that the genuinely needy—at present very ill-served—receive the resources they are due, and which should be a matter of entitlement for them. Nor is the reintegration of the underclass in society likely to occur. Instead, we will be left with a wasteful and invasive Leviathan, whose resources are squandered on middle-class subsidies generated by collusive interest groups and by the operation of the vote motive, and which leaves those truly vulnerable to their own devices.[93] An ambitious goal, but one achievable over the long haul by administrations committed to limited government with a positive responsibility to the satisfaction of basic needs and the conservation of the common culture, would be the reduction of state expenditure to around a quarter of national product, as advocated by Hayek.[94] Such a goal, though it would amount to a transformation of government little short of revolutionary, will not satisfy fundamentalist advocates of *laissez-faire*, but it is probably one that no British government will for the foreseeable future even approach, given the inheritance of earlier interventionist policies (including an increase of the portion of national product appropriated by government to around 38 percent) and the political memory of ill-conceived measures which reduced government expenditure without due regard to their human costs and the impact of such cuts on established expectations. It is the argument of this chapter that, given that over a decade of policy aimed at reducing the role of government in society has resulted in an increase of state expenditure as a proportion of national product, and in which state activity is in absolute terms probably higher than ever before, a genuine and lasting reduction in the size, cost and invasiveness of the state is to be achieved only by a revision and revaluation of the agenda of government in which its positive responsibilities are clearly and explicitly specified.

8

Conclusion

The argument of this paper is that, once market socialism has been struck off the policy agenda, the spectrum of reasoned debate that remains extends at most—at least in Britain, and other similar modern states—from unconstrained libertarian capitalism at one end to egalitarian social democracy at the other. More radically, I have argued that neither extreme of that spectrum can be given a compelling ethical or philosophical rationale. Both libertarianism and egalitarianism lack credibility as fundamental political moralities, and for that reason should also be removed from the intellectual and political agenda. The real space for reasoned debate is much narrower than the spectrum so conceived, even though both ends of it accept the necessity in a modern economy of free market institutions and of the institution of private property in the means of production on which effective market pricing depends. The real space for public discourse is not between the two extremes, but in the area of detailed debate about the scope and content of public goods, the depth and limits of the common culture, the relative costs of government failure and market failure, and the content and levels of provision of basic needs. This is the agenda of policy that should inform public discourse henceforth, and upon which political consensus in Britain should in future be established.

A liberal civil society cannot hope to be stable if political life is polarized between ideological extremes. If the argument of this paper is sound, the ideologies of libertarian capitalism and egalitarian social democracy lack any persuasive defence in ethical or philosophical terms. Abandoning these doctrinaire positions does *not* mean adopting a middle ground of muddled pragmatism: it means occupying the only real space for disciplined reasoning. For conservatives in Britain, such a move entails abandoning the simplistic formulae and utopian panaceas of the libertarian New Right and recognising the dependency of the market economy on a common culture containing institutions that protect those whom the unconstrained market would neglect. Such a recognition need not prove difficult for conservatives who have not forgotten the communitarian concerns of traditional Toryism and who know something of the achievements and policies of Christian Democratic governments in Europe. For British social democrats, the move toward a new consensus means shedding the disabling illusions of egalitarianism in order to consider the detailed failings of the market and of the current welfare state. The example given by the European social-democratic parties, especially in Germany and Austria, should make this move more easily negotiable. It would be a hopeful augury for liberal civil society in Britain if, by the abandonment of fundamentalist positions in the major parties, a new consensus were to emerge that facilitated civilised public, political discourse about the agenda and limits of governmental intervention in society and the economy. It is such a space of convergence or consensus, with all its variations and disagreements, that I have tried to stake out under the general category of the social market economy, and the particular example of the enabling welfare state.

In its critical application to neo-liberal thought and policy, the argument has been that an individualist order is not free-standing, but depends on forms of common life for its worth and its very existence. Equally, autonomy is valueless if it is exercised in a community denuded of the inherently public goods that create worthwhile options and which thereby make good choices possible. One of the basic needs of human beings is membership in a community. Such membership will be stable if, and only if, the community is seen to be meeting basic human needs, through the institutions of the market, and, where these fail, through other institutions, such as the enabling welfare state.

The morality of the market is one that prizes and rewards integrity and responsibility. It is one that has as its ultimate ethical justification the role of the vital interest in autonomy in individual human well-being. The morality of the market is the only morality consistent with the reproduction of a liberal civilisation. Defenders of this morality must acknowledge that a principled commitment to its values carries with it, logically, morally and politically, a commitment to measures that protect the well-being and autonomy of the vulnerable and the defence-less. A market economy without this commitment lacks both ethical and political legitimacy. It is the argument of this paper that a humane social market economy is the only sort of free economy likely to survive in the years to come, and the only sort that deserves to survive.

Notes

1 On this, see J. Kornai, 'The Hungarian Reform Process', *Journal of Economic Literature, XXIV,* (4), December 1986.

2 For an introduction to public choice theory, see James Buchanan and Gordon Tullock, *The Calculus of Consent,* Ann Arbor: University of Michigan Press, 1962.

3 See Hayek, *Individualism and Economic Order,* London and Henley, Routledge and Kegan Paul, 1976, Chapters II, IV, VII-IX. For an excellent history of the Austrian calculation debate, see D. Lavoie, *Rivalry and Central Planning: the Socialist Calculation Debate Reconsidered,* Cambridge: Cambridge University Press, 1985.

4 Michael Polanyi, *The Logic of Liberty,* Chicago: University of Chicago Press, 1951.

5 Paul Craig Roberts, *Alienation and the Soviet Economy: the Collapse of the Socialist Era,* 2nd edition, New York and London: Holmes and Meier, 1990.

6 G.L.S. Shackle, *Epistemics and Economics,* Cambridge: Cambridge University Press, 1972.

7 I owe this formulation to Michael Oakeshott, *Rationalism in Politics,* London and New York: Methuen, 1977.

8 G.L.S. Shackle, *Epistemics and Economics: a critique of economic doctrine,* Cambridge: Cambridge University Press, 1972, p. 239.

9 Shackle, *ibid.,* p. 240.

10 James Buchanan, 'Jack Wiseman: A Personal Appreciation', in *Constitutional Political Economy,* Vol. 2, No. 1, Winter 1991, p. 4.

11 Insofar as Austrian economic theory neglects, or seeks always to explain away as by-products of government intervention, the endogenous breakdowns of coordination in markets theorised by Keynes and Shackle, it becomes seriously misleading.

12 See, also, Peter Rutland, *The Myth of the Plan,* London: Hutchinson, 1985; and James Sherr, *Soviet Power: the Continuing Challenge,* London: Macmillan, 1987, pp. 27-30.

13 As I shall note later, it is far from being the case that Soviet military technology is uniformly less advanced than that in the West: on the contrary, with the important exception of some of the computer technologies that go into space-based defense systems, it is often in advance of its Western counterparts.

14 For a decisive demolition of this species of rationalism, see Michael Oakeshott, *Rationalism in Politics,* London: Methuen, 1962, p. 96, footnote et. seq.

15 On this, see A. Narrozov, *The Coming Order: Reflections on Sovietology and the Media,* Claridge Blast no. 4, London: Claridge Press, 1991, p.12.

16 For further evidence on this point, see my paper, *The Strange Death of Perestroika: Causes and Consequences of the Soviet Coup,* European Security Studies No. 13, London: Institute of European Defence and Strategic Studies, 1991, pp. 20-21.

17 A. Alchian, 'Uncertainty, Evolution and Economic Theory', *Journal of Political Economy,* 58, pp. 211-222, 1950; H.G. Manne, 'Mergers and the Market for Corporate Control', *Journal of Political Economy,* 73, 1965, pp. 110-120; S.G. Winter, 'Satisficing, Selection and the Innovative Element', *Quarterly Journal of Economics,* 83, 1971, pp. 237-261; P. Pelikan, 'Evolution, Economic Competence, and the Market for Corporate Control', *Journal of Economic Behaviour and Organization,* 12, 1989, pp. 279-303.

18 Pelikan, *op. cit.,* pp. 281-282.

19 An unfettered market for corporate control may have negative as well as positive effects on the economy. The German and the Japanese examples suggest that market competition may not be inhibited, and long-term planning facilitated, by an environment where stock market fluctuations are less important in their impact on firms than in Anglo-American style economies. This is an important point I cannot pursue here.

20 I take this to be Raymond Plant's view, as expressed in his contribution to *Citizenship and Rights in Thatcher's Britain: Two Views*, Raymond Plant and Norman Barry, London: IEA Health and Welfare Unit, 1990, and in Plant's Fabian Society pamphlets, *Equality, Markets and the State*, (Fabian Tract 494, January, 1984) and *Citizenship, Rights and Idealism*, (Fabian Society Tract 531, October 1988).

21 For an argument that it often does not, see E. J. Mishan, *The Costs of Economic Growth*, London: Pelican, 1967.

22 G.L.S. Shackle, *Epistemics and Economics: A Critique of Economic Doctrines*, Cambridge: Cambridge University Press, 1972.

23 I have myself stated this objection, more systematically, in my *Liberalisms: Essays in Political Philosophy*, London: Routledge, 1989, Chapter 12.

24 For the best untechnical discussion of value-incommensurability, see Isaiah Berlin, 'On the Pursuit of the Ideal', in *The Crooked Timber of Humanity: Chapters in the History of Ideas*, John Murray, London: 1990.

25 For a good statement of this view, see David G. Green, *Equalizing People*, London: IEA Health and Welfare Unit, Choice in Welfare Series No. 4, Chapter Four.

26 On Berlin, see my 'On Negative and Positive Liberty', in my *Liberalisms, ibid.*, Chapter Four.

27 For a comprehensive argument that negative liberty has little or no intrinsic value, see Joseph Raz, *The Morality of Freedom*, Oxford: Clarendon Press, 1986, Chapters 14 and 15.

28 Raz, *ibid.*, p. 207. I have myself argued for a conception of freedom as autonomy in my *Liberalism*, Milton Keynes: Open University Press, 1986, pp. 58-61.

29 See Hirschman's *Exit, Voice and Loyalty*, Cambridge, Mass:, Harvard University Press, 1970.

30 F.A. Hayek, *The Constitution of Liberty*, London: Routledge and Kegan Paul, 1960.

31 See Joel Feinberg, *Moral Limits of the Criminal Law*, Vol. 2, *Harm to Self*, Oxford: Oxford University Press, 1986, Chapter 18.

32 See Loren Lomasky, *Rights, Persons and the Moral Community*, Oxford: Oxford University Press, 1987, pp. 247-250.

33 See Raz, *ibid.*, Chapters 14 and 15.

34 For a critique of Rawlsian legalism, see my *Liberalisms, ibid.*, Chapter 10.

35 On this, see my *Liberalisms, ibid.*, postscript.

36 See Plant's contribution to *Citizenship and Rights in Thatcher's Britain:Two Views*, London: IEA Health and Welfare Unit, Choice in Welfare Series No. 3, 1990, especially pp. 20-22.

37 Raz, *ibid.*, Chapter 9.

38 Raz, *ibid.*, p. 235.

39 Raz, *ibid.*, 240.

40 L.P. Hartley, *Facial Justice*, Oxford: Oxford University Press, 1987.

41 F.A. Hayek, *The Constitution of Liberty*, Chicago: Henry Regnery, 1960, pp. 90-91; R. Nozick, *Anarchy, State and Utopia*, Oxford: Basil Blackwell, 1974, pp. 167-168.

42 On this, see Bruno Bettelheim, *The Children of the Dream*, London and New York.

43 F.A. Hayek, *The Constitution of Liberty*, p. 87.

44 On this, see my *Mill on Liberty: A Defence*, London: Routledge, 1983, Chapter Three.

45 From the standpoint of the present argument, according to which 'justice' is a short-hand term for a miscellany of practices and procedures having in common only a regulative ideal of fairness, there cannot be a *theory* of justice—though there can be a theory of law.

46 J.S. Mill, 'On Liberty', in John Gray, (ed), *Four Essays*, Oxford: Oxford University Press, 1991, p. 87.

47 F.A. Hayek, *The Constitution of Liberty*, Chapter 6.

96

48 F.A. Hayek, *Law, Legislation and Liberty*, vol. 2, *The Mirage of Social Justice*, London: Routledge and Keegan Paul, (one volume edition), 1982, pp. 115-120.

49 See Mill's, *Principles of Political Economy*, London: Penguin edition, 1970, p. 350. '...the distribution of wealth. That is a matter of human institution only. The things once there, mankind, individually or collectively, can do with them as they like.'

50 See B. de Jouvenel, *Ethics of Redistribution*, Indianapolis: Liberty Press, 1990, Introduction by John Gray.

51 On this, see D.K. Willis, *Klass: How Russians Really Live*, New York: St. Martin's Press, 1985.

52 See Hayek's *Individualism and Economic Order, ibid.* I have discussed Hayek's argument in my *Hayek on Liberty*, Oxford: Basil Blackwell, pp. 13-16, 21-26.

53 David Miller, *Market, State and Community: Theoretical Foundations of Market Socialism*, Oxford: Clarendon Press, 1989.

54 For Mill's 'competitive syndicalism', see his *Principles of Political Economy*, London: Penguin edition, 1970, pp. 118-141.

55 On this, see A. Schuller, *Does Market Socialism Work*, London: Centre for Research into Communist Economies; and V.A. Naishul, *The Supreme and Last Stage of Socialism*, London: Centre for Research into Communist Economies.

56 For the best statement of this analytical Marxist critique of classical Marxist conception of exploitation and alienation, see G.A. Cohen, *History, Labour and Freedom: Themes from Marx*, Oxford: Clarendon Press, 1988, Chapters 6-9.

57 See Miller, *ibid.*, Chapter Three.

58 R. Nozick, *Anarchy, State and Utopia*, Oxford: Basil Blackwell, 1974, p. 163.

59 For a brilliant discussion of this and other aspects of neutrality, see Raz, *ibid.*, Chapter Five.

60 Gerald F. Gaus, 'A Contractual Justification of Redistributive Capitalism', p. 111. Gaus also notes (p. 121, footnote 89) that the oft-cited Mondragon cooperative in Spain generates adequate levels of income 'only because of its very special circumstances, in particular its nonmobile labour force'. See Keith Bradley and Alan Gelb, 'The Replication and Sustainability of the Mondragon Experiment', *British Journal of Industrial Relations*, 20, 1982, pp. 20-33. If immobility is a precondition of worker-cooperative viability, what becomes of the freedom of workers?

61 Miller, 'Market Neutrality and the Failure of Co-operatives', *British Journal of Political Science*, 11, 1981, p. 328.

62 Some of these difficulties have been acknowledged by Miller in 'A Vision of Market Socialism', *Dissent*, Summer 1991, pp. 406-415.

63 Anthony de Jasay, *Market Socialism: A Scrutiny: 'This Square Circle'*, London: IEA Occasional Paper 84, 1990, p. 21.

64 See, in particular, Walter Lippman, *The Good Society*, Boston: 1937; and H. Simon, *Economic Policy for a Free Society*, Chicago: University of Chicago Press, 1948.

65 A. M. Honore, 'Ownership', in A. G. Guest, *Oxford Essays in Jurisprudence 1*, Oxford: Oxford University Press, 1961.

66 James Buchanan, 'Tacit preoppositions of political economy: implications for societies in transition', (unpublished).

67 Norman Barry, *Welfare*, Milton Keynes: Open University Press, 1990, pp. 78-82.

68 The term compossibility is owed to Hillel Steiner, but originates in Leibniz's monadology. See H. Steiner, 'The Structure of a Set of Compossible Rights', *Journal of Philosophy*, 1977; and, on non-conflictability, Joel Feinberg, *Social Philosophy*, Englewood Cliffs, New Jersey: Prentice-Hall, 1973, pp. 95-96.

69 This is a point acknowledged by Barry, *ibid.*, p. 79.

70 See H.L.A. Hart, *The Concept of Law*, Oxford: Clarendon Press, 1961, pp. 184-195.

71 Raz, *ibid.*, Chapters Seven and Eight. It may be worth noting that the welfare state could be given a derivation in contractarian terms. For an example of this, see Christopher Morris, *A Hobbesian Welfare State?*, *Dialogue XXVII* (1988), pp. 653-673.

72 See Raz, *ibid.*, pp. 235-244.

73 See my *Limited Government, ibid.*

74 See my *A conservative disposition, ibid.*, p. 27.

75 Raz, *ibid.*, p. 242.

76 I developed this argument myself in 'Classical Liberalism, Positional Goods, and the Politicisation of Poverty', in *Dilemmas of Liberal Democracy*, (ed.) A. Ellis and E. Kumar, London: Tavistock, 1983, pp. 174-184.

77 Raz, *ibid.*, p. 242.

78 In my *Limited Government: A Positive Agenda, ibid.*

79 See my *Advertising Bans: Administrative Decisions or Matters of Principle?* London: Social Affairs Unit, 1991.

80 See, on this, K. R. Popper, *The Open Society and Its Enemies*, Vol. 1, London: Routledge and Kegan Paul, Chapter 9.

81 Raz, *ibid.*, Chapters Fourteen and Fifteen.

82 For a perfectionist defense of liberalism, see V. Haksar, *Liberty, Equality and Perfectionism*, Oxford: Oxford University Press, 1979.

83 On this, see my *Limited Government*, p. 74.

84 The term wanton originates with H.G. Frankfurt and is explained in my *Mill on Liberty: A Defence*, p. 75.

85 On this, see my *A Conservative Disposition, ibid.*, pp. 21-22. See, also, David Willett's excellent *Happy Families: four points to a Conservative family policy*, London: Centre for Policy Studies, Policy Study 120, 1991.

86 Raz, *ibid.*, p. 309.

87 See Hayek's *Monetary Nationalism and International Stability*, London: Longmans, Green, 1937. I have earlier argued for Hayekian currency competition on the ground that money may in the conditions of the contemporary British economy be unmeasurable: see my *Limited Government, op. cit.*, pp. 45-48. I have since been convinced by the arguments of Tim Congdon that this Hayekian objection to monetarist policy is unfounded. On this see T. Congdon, *Monetarism Lost: and Why it Must be Regained*, London: Centre for Policy Studies, May 1989.

88 See T.W. Hutchinson, *The Politics and Philosophy of Economics: Marxists, Keynesians and Austrians*, Oxford: Basil Blackwell, 1981, Chapter Five, 'Walter Eucken and the German Social-Market Economies', pp. 154-175. See also, Lord Keith Joseph, *The Social Market Economy*, London: Centre for Policy Studies.

89 Hutchinson, *op. cit.*, p. 162.

90 Hutchinson, *op. cit.*, p. 168.

91 Hutchinson, *op.cit.*, p. 17.

92 The spirit of the German Social Market Economy School has been well captured by E.Y. Neaman, who observes:

> It was hardly a coincidence that behind Ludwig Erhard's concept of a *Sozialmarktwirtschaft* (social market economy) lay the conservative cultural criticism of capitalism of Erhard's mentor, the philosopher Alfred Müller-Armack. In an influential book of the era, *Diagnosis of Our Times* (1949), Müller-Armack pleaded for a synthesis of two opposing forces: the ruthlessness of the market and the Christian concept of brotherly love. Müller-Armack's stress on the *social* side of the market equation typifies the general ambiguity of the German liberals in the postwar period. The founders of the social market economy, known as the "Ordo" group, after the economic journal of that name, were sceptical of unhindered market

capitalism. Thinkers like Wilhelm Röpke and Alexander Rüstow advocated a social market as a collective healing process, by which social harmony should be instituted and traditional values, such as the sanctity of the family and Christian morality, preserved. Even the so-called Freibourg Group, economists who were more pragmatic and politically minded, saw the social market as a kind of objective mechanism which would regulate the collective in the most efficacious manner. They were not opposed to government intervention as long as its aim was to make competition even more effective. Thus, for example, government subsidies for the poor to pay rent were seen as enforcing the social market, but rent control was not.

The 'social state' (*Sozialstaat*, the same appellation used by Gottfried Feder) was built on four fundamental pillars after 1945: (1) old-age pensions; (2) health and accident insurance; (3) employment-creation and unemployment insurance; and (4) family support.... In contrast to the past, the Basic Law (*Grundgesetz*) of 1949, which is the closest the Federal Republic has to a constitution, made the state responsible for protecting its citizens from social insecurity.

E.A. Neaman, 'German Collectivism and the Welfare State', *Critical Review*, vol. 4, number 4, Fall 1990, pp. 607-8. The point is that, the social market economy model conferred on citizens an entitlement to protection from insecurity.

93 For evidence on this point, see Julien Le Grand, *The Strategy of Equality*, London: 1984.

94 F.A. Hayek, *The Constitution of Liberty*, London: 1960, p. 323.

Commentaries

Freedom versus Autonomy

Chandran Kukathas

Is economic coordination possible without central direction? In the nineteenth century a series of European writers answered 'no', and insisted that, at best, markets coordinated imperfectly. Without intervention, imperfection would manifest itself in the form of wasteful over-production, the rise and collapse of firms driven by the whims of fashion, and unemployment. The product of all this could only be social dislocation and anomie. Out of such convictions were born the command economies of twentieth-century Europe.

Half a century of economic planning has left the idea of central direction discredited. In his revisionary essay, *The Moral Foundations of Market Institutions*, John Gray makes it clear that, indeed, there was never a convincing intellectual justification for central economic control.

Yet while the case for economic planning has been vanquished, the clamour for some form of social control has not disappeared. In the absence of central direction, it is contended, free individuals will coordinate imperfectly and fail to produce such vital goods as welfare, culture and science. This is an argument which requires some attention. It is advanced by John Gray to bolster his contention that libertarian variants of liberalism are defective, and to establish that the only plausible liberal political philosophy is one which finds a middle way between the extremes of socialism and classical liberalism.

My purpose here is to examine and criticize John Gray's argument from the perspective of a classical liberal. Since others will wish to question different aspects of his theory, let me begin by identifying what I regard as central to Gray's position, before turning to offer a substantive critique. My ambition is to lure the stray philosopher back into the liberal extremist fold.

Gray's philosophical defence of the middle way turns upon an assertion about the importance of *autonomy*, its preservation and its distribution. Two kinds of argument are offered: first, a negative argument about the classical liberal view of freedom, which is condemned as indeterminate at best and, at worst, incoherent; and second, a positive argument about the value of autonomy.

Gray's negative argument maintains that classical liberals have no plausible answer to the question of what is intrinsically valuable about the negative freedom of absence of coercion. Moreover, the content of negative liberty is always 'radically indeterminate'. From this we must conclude, Gray maintains, that the value of negative liberty must 'be theorized in terms of its contribution to something other than itself, which does possess intrinsic value' (p. 22)—and that something is the positive liberty of *autonomy*. The autonomous person is one 'who is self-possessed, who has a distinct self-identity or individuality, who is authentic and self-directed, and whose life is to some significant degree a matter of self-creation' (p. 25). Autonomy is vital if we, in the West at least, are to lead valuable lives.

From here Gray goes on to argue that our concern must be to ensure that the conditions which make autonomy possible are preserved. This means that individuals must be assured of access to the resources needed for a life that is at least partly self-directed, and steps must be taken to preserve the public culture that makes autonomy possible. While market institutions are vital if this is to be achieved, it is equally important that individuals be given welfare rights, and that the public culture be protected from the ravages of the market.

My response to Gray's argument embraces three general claims. First, the classical liberal idea of freedom is not incoherent; nor is its indeterminacy the problem Gray alleges it is. Second, autonomy may be an important value, but it is not as important as he maintains. Third, however important autonomy may be, this does not justify the institutions of central social planning that Gray's proposals ultimately defend.

Classical Liberalism and Negative Liberty

Let us begin by considering the classical liberal idea of (negative) freedom. While there are many variants of classical liberalism, they share the view that liberty is enjoyed by individuals to the extent that their activities are not constrained or interfered with. The problem has always been to explain what counts as a constraint or interference which restricts liberty. After all, rules of property might be regarded as restrictions on liberty since they render individuals unfree to do many things—like trespassing or stealing. Indeed, all systems of rules create opportunities and impose constraints upon those who work within them. So when can we rightly complain about loss of liberty?

Many attempts to meet the challenge this question poses—classical liberal attempts included—have been found wanting. But does this mean that all such attempts are without value, if not entirely pointless? Gray suggests so, claiming that classical liberalism has no good answer to the question of why negative liberty understood in terms of the absence of coercion is intrinsically valuable. But he is mistaken: there is a reason why negative liberty is valuable. Free actions are *my* actions. Infringements of my negative liberty make some of my actions no longer my own; if serious and extensive enough, they make my activities—or even my life—no longer my own. Restrictions on my liberty (which, say, close off particular options) restrict the fulfilment of *my* desires. This is not to say that objects or activities can have no value in themselves. But many things have value only because we seek them; they cannot have value if we cannot seek them; and they will not be valued by us if we are forced to gain them. They have value because we are free to seek them, and seek them freely.

Nothing in this argument appeals to autonomy. This needs to be emphasised because it may look as if I am conceding to Gray that the value of negative liberty lies in its contribution to autonomy. But I am not. What I am arguing is that many actions and activities acquire value because we are free to undertake them and undertake them freely. It is not essential, however, that we choose to do so autonomously. The action may not be that of an 'authentic', 'self-directed' person involved in a process of 'self-creation'; it may be thoughtless and ill-considered. It may still have value, however, because it is *my* action, an expression of *my* preference. Consider the case of a soccer hooligan, who spends most of his waking hours drunk and most of his sober hours asleep. When alert enough to express a preference he tells us he likes to attend Arsenal's matches (to hurl abuse at opposing fans). When asked if he has nothing better to do he replies, 'What do you mean?' A less autonomous person would be hard to find. Yet he would suffer a loss if forced one weekend (by a gang of hooligans) to go to a Chelsea match; he values going to Arsenal because he has always hurled abuse at Highbury and not at Stamford Bridge. The infringement of his liberty has made his activity worthless to him, though it has not occasioned any loss of autonomy.

Many of our own activities, while perhaps not as degenerate as those of our soccer hooligan, do not reflect any degree of autonomy. They are the product of whimsy rather than reflection; caprice rather than deliberation; random selection rather than choice. Yet they are still free and have value to us. If I decide, on impulse, to go (again) to see *Rocky IV* at the movies but am denied admission (by a policeman who fancies himself as a film critic), I suffer a loss of liberty—and value—which may not be compensated by a free ticket to see *Citizen Cane* playing next door. This infringement of my negative liberty is a bad thing, but not because autonomy is in any way involved.

The argument here is not, however, to suggest that negative liberty is a good because 'it facilitates the satisfaction of wants'. This position, as Gray rightly notes, would 'license the abridgement of negative freedom whenever want-satisfaction is thereby increased' (p. 21). I am not arguing that liberty helps to maximize want-satisfaction. My claim is, rather, that negative liberty is essential if many of our wants and desires are to have value. What makes our wants and desires valuable is the fact that they are *our* wants and desires; to respect negative liberty is to respect this attachment.

Yet even if it is conceded that negative liberty can be intrinsically valuable, what of Gray's complaint that we have no agreed procedure for measuring and weighing on-balance freedom? This, he suggests, means that the idea that negative freedom is a value that should be maximized or optimized breaks down completely. But this does not matter if one takes the view that negative freedom is a value which is to be honoured or respected rather than promoted or maximized. Indeed the issue of freedom cannot sensibly turn on the question of the *amount* of freedom in one society as against another. In some societies groups of individuals may choose to restrict their options and so limit their liberty (say by joining a church which proscribes certain forms of behaviour). In other societies such individuals may be denied the freedom to form or join churches. Even if we could measure the amount of liberty enjoyed in each of these two societies and found that in the former people had more options, it would still be the case that the latter is the free society.

All this is, of course, quite 'indeterminate'; indeed, according to Gray, the content of negative liberty is *radically* indeterminate'. Now if by this he means that we cannot, from a principle enjoining respect for negative liberty, derive a definitive set of entitlements and prohibitions on individual and institutional conduct, he is perfectly correct. But I fail to see why this is a serious objection. Political theory does not end with the assertion of a set of principles; political argument and moral reasoning must still continue; principles have to be interpreted and interpretations have to be defended. Social theory generally is 'indeterminate'. We should indeed accept Aristotle's wise suggestion that we not look for more precision than a subject will allow.

If, however, Gray means that the idea of negative liberty can do *nothing* to help us distinguish acceptable from unacceptable conduct, his view seems to me simply implausible. A principle requiring respect for liberty would, at the very least, prohibit blowing up the freedom-loving peoples of Britain. It would also tell us that a range of other less extravagant activities were not acceptable—imprisoning the innocent, silencing dissenters, persecuting infidels. Of course, in all these cases arguments would have to be made for advancing particular conclusions; but a principle of liberty would still play a pivotal role, filtering out certain kinds of considerations as irrelevant if liberty is to be valued and upheld.

Negative liberty is undoubtedly an important value, and classical liberals are right to place great store by it. It is not the only value; but this is not to deny its importance. John Gray, I fear, has underestimated its importance, just as he has overrated the value of autonomy.

The Value of Autonomy

By 'autonomy' Gray means 'the condition in which a person can be at least part author of his life, in that he has before him a range of worthwhile options, in respect of which his choices are not fettered by coercion and with regard to which he possesses the capacities and resources presupposed by a reasonable measure of success in his self-chosen path among these options' (p. 22). The crucial part of this definition is the first, which emphasises the importance of a person being 'part author' of his life. The remainder of the definition tries to indicate what makes for such authorship.

The problem, however, is to specify the extent to which a person must be the author of his life to qualify as autonomous. Consider, for example, the case of the slave-hero, Tom, in Harriet Beecher Stowe's novel, *Uncle Tom's Cabin*. A slave since birth, Tom nonetheless has an assuredness and self-control born of deep Christian conviction. To his new master's promise to possess him 'body and soul' Tom replies that his owner may do what he will with his body, but not his soul—which belongs to another. Tom's independence of spirit contrasts sharply with the pitiable character of his owner, Simon Legree. For all his confident brutality, he is revealed to be the prisoner of his own upbringing, tormented by superstitious fears, with little capacity to shape or give meaning to his life.

According to Gray's definition, it would seem that the slave-owner here qualifies as autonomous: he has a range of worthwhile options (though he chooses badly); he is not coerced; and he has the capacities and resources to pursue worthwhile ends. Tom has none of these things and so cannot qualify as autonomous. Yet this cannot be correct; it is, in this instance, the slave who is autonomous.

The point here is that there is a certain vagueness about the idea of autonomy which makes it of dubious value as a standard. Since the key to autonomy is self-direction or self-authorship it has to be admitted that autonomy depends a good deal on one's character and state of mind. Whether or not one becomes autonomous will therefore depend on the factors which build one's character. Having resources and being free from coercion may be important for one to be able to *exercise* that autonomy in certain ways; but these things do not make one autonomous. Indeed, it is a mark of an autonomous person that he is able to make the most of what few resources and opportunities he has. Gray appears to recognize that autonomy may be the product of many things when he notes that 'autonomy is a complex status, not definable by reference to the presence or absence of any single condition' (p. 22). But he does not then draw what I would suggest is the most likely conclusion, that the notion of autonomy is too indeterminate in its nature to give us much help. Indeed, so many things could make people autonomous that it is hard to see why Gray thinks that the market has a special place as an 'enabling device' fostering autonomy.

Now Gray may want to object that I have misconstrued what he means by autonomy. After all, he does say that autonomy also requires that people not be coerced and have a range of worthwhile options.[1] But these are essentially requirements of negative liberty. What distinguishes autonomy from mere negative liberty is the insistence on the significance of self-direction. It is here, however, that the notion becomes fuzzy and indeterminate. What does it mean for someone to be 'self-possessed', or to be 'authentic and self-directed'; if an autonomous life must be 'to some significant degree a matter of self-creation', how far does it have to be self-created (assuming it is clear what 'self-creation' means)? If a life is not self-created simply because it is uncoerced and its possessor has a range of options to choose from, what exactly is a self-created life?

Yet this may be too harsh. It may be that the core of the notion of autonomy has a meaning which is clearer and less inaccessible than I am making out. Nonetheless, I would maintain that this ideal of self-direction is less worthy than is imagined. If autonomy denotes a certain quality of mind—a resilience, or fortitude, or 'self-possession'—it has to be noted that this is not always a good thing. One might be autonomous in the sense that one has the mental qualities needed to put up with, or make the most of, one's lot; yet more good might come if people were less able to cope with and more inclined to *react* against their circumstances.

Simon Leys recounts the story of Lu Hsün's response to Bertrand Russell who, like many foreign visitors to China, was struck with admiration by the capacity of the Chinese to 'enrich all the events of life, even the most irksome and most barren, and make something savory out of them'.[2] Russell had written: 'I remember one hot day when a party of us were crossing the hills in chairs—the way was rough and very steep, the work for the coolies very severe. At the highest point of our journey, we stopped for ten minutes to let the men rest. Instantly they all sat in a row, brought out their pipes, and began to laugh among themselves as if they had not a care in the world'. On this Lu Hsün remarked: 'As for Russell, who praises the Chinese after seeing smiling porters at the Western Lake, I do not know exactly what he is driving at. I do know one thing: if the porters had been able not to smile at those whom they carried, China would have long since been out of its present rut'.[3]

The ideal of autonomy is the ideal of the intellectual. It is the ideal of those who stress the importance of our *rational* faculties: our capacity of reflect, to deliberate, to 'choose'. These abilities are undoubtedly a part of our make-up; but only a part. Most of our pursuits are not the product of rational deliberation; nor are they 'chosen' in any sense other than that they are the result of voluntary action. Though it would be going too far to say that we are simply constituted or determined by our social context, it would not be to say that we tend to prefer, to value, to attach ourselves to the familiar and the attractive. Such inclinations are not rational but emotional; and we worry less about whether we are self-directed than about whether we are obstructed.

The upholder of autonomy often forgets that people are too busy living their lives to worry about directing it; too often he remembers, and exercises his ingenuity looking for ways of forcing them to be autonomous. At worst, this involves doing violence to the actual practices and lives people pursue; at best, it means paternalistic action to 'create the conditions' which make autonomy possible—though it has to be asked how autonomous one can be if someone else takes charge of the task of ensuring that possibility.

We should be wary of those who peddle autonomy, for we risk trading away our liberties to the people who promise to preserve them. Indeed, this is the upshot of many of the practical proposals put forward by John Gray in the name of liberty as autonomy.

Planning for Liberty?

If we are concerned about individual autonomy and human welfare, Gray suggests, the philosophies of libertarians or laissez-faire liberals must be discarded. We must go the way of the 'social market economy', underpinned by strong welfare rights and clearly specified government duties to preserve the culture which make such a market economy possible. While economic planning is out, central social planning is vital to preserve the cultural basis of our economic institutions, to uphold individual autonomy, and protect certain intrinsic goods.

There are two kinds of reservations a classical liberal might express about Gray's argument. The first concerns the move from an assertion that certain values or ends are desirable to the conclusion that it should be government's task to promote them. The second concerns the neglect of individual liberty that these conclusions presage.

The market, Gray notes, is not a 'natural datum' but 'an extremely complex artifact' (p. 28). It is not what remains when regulations have been removed but a legal construct. This is a point that Hayek makes very vigorously in his essay, '"Free" Enterprise and Competitive Order',[4] and which I think, contrary to Gray, most liberals recognize as uncontroversial. The question is, what kinds of legal institutions and laws are called for. Gray's answer is that they must be institutions and laws which do more than simply protect individual negative liberty; they must be institutions which have a more positive role—or, more precisely which specify a more interventionist role for government. The problem with the case that Gray puts, however, is that it does not offer replies to long-standing classical-liberal criticisms of such interventionism. The most general criticism has been that intervention will not achieve its intended objectives.

Consider the assertion that government should aim to provide its citizens with 'a guarantee of the resources and opportunities required for the autonomous pursuit of the good life' (p. 57). The practical objection classical liberals have usually raised is that, granting the moral premise, governments generally have failed to do any such thing. Gray himself maintains that, in Britain, welfare is a wasteful 'middle-class racket' (p. 87). Yet the only practical solution suggested to this problem is that we should seek to eliminate or reduce such waste (p. 85). But this surely will not do; every opposition party seeking government promises to root out inequities, to find hitherto undiscovered efficiencies and to cut waste. These are fantasies of the well-meaning. If centralized control of welfare-provision is to be defended, it would be far better to admit that there will be enormous waste which is justified by the successful meeting of basic welfare aims. That in itself will be a tall order.

A more serious problem still is that systems of centralized welfare produce large and intrusive welfare bureaucracies. Gray's proposals for welfare rights recognize this inasmuch as they are intended to deliver their holders from discretionary authority (p. 70). Yet while such measures as vouchers to give greater discretionary power to individuals are to be welcomed as an improvement, they will ultimately do little to weaken the bureaucratic apparatus needed to maintain them.[5] In the final analysis, the problem is that all such schemes have to be administered; and no system of administrative law is going to monitor and check appropriately the activities of administrative agencies.

On top of this we would retain many of the inefficiencies associated with centralized distribution mechanisms—notably that of the misallocation of resources. Hospital closures and queues for routine medical services will continue to come hand in hand with problems of 'overuse'.[6]

The other important respect in which Gray sees an important role for the government is what might be termed cultural policy. He maintains, very plausibly, that for individuals to be able to make certain kinds of choices and have certain kinds of options, there must be a special kind of cultural environment. What is less plausible is his move to the conclusion that this gives the state particular responsibilities. State support and subsidy of some of the arts, for example, is not defensible simply on the ground that they are intrinsically valuable. If activities are intrinsically valuable there is a good chance that people will engage in them or support those who do. Some activities may do badly because people do not think them worthwhile; there is no reason to allow those few who think these worth supporting to force their fellow taxpayers to pay for them. None of this implies any kind of value-scepticism, as Gray suggests; we simply have to accept that people may choose badly. One reason we should accept this is that we have no reason whatsoever to think that government instrumentalities will choose well. Those of us who look with alarm, if not horror, at the way in which Shakespeare and Dickens have been eased out of many a state school syllabus, suspect that they will usually choose badly. Cultural standards are important; but this is all the more reason to take them out of the control of government.

Further to this there is also the question of *how much* of such goods should be provided. In the arts and the sciences government provision means that the base level of support for these activities is centrally determined—and the fear of some is, presumably, that without such provision the level of support will be too low. One problem here is that we simply do not know to what extent 'pure research', for example, will be sustained without subsidy. But the bigger question is, how much 'pure research' should there be? At what point would the supply be too low to make for an appropriately rich cultural environment. In the absence of a reasonable answer to this question, it is hard to see how any case for subsidy or support can be made.

All these considerations were raised to make the point that Gray's move from the importance of certain values to the necessity of governmental responsibility is not defensible. My other concern is that, in many cases such recommendations lead to loss of liberty. Gray is insightful in his recognition of the importance of intermediary institutions, such as the family. But in maintaining that a 'liberal government has a positive responsibility to tend and nurture' them (p. 78), he neglects the possibility that it is the extension of governmental responsibility that has tended to undermine them. The family is a case in point. On a number of occasions Gray appeals to the success of Swedish policy (on labour, for example—p. 80). Yet one of the 'problems' in Sweden is the erosion of the family as the result of many of its responsibilities being taken away from it. (I will not dwell on the question of individual responsibility, since the important points are made by Gray in his critique of egalitarianism in Chapter 4.) Here we find exceptionally high levels of divorce and single-parenthood.

A similar story might be told about other kinds of associations. Governments taking a positive interest in institutions such as universities has tended to undermine them, and to distract them from those activities and pursuits which are their *raison d'etre*. This tends to threaten freedom inasmuch as these institutions would otherwise be harbours or shelters for individuals interested in particular pursuits. Without genuinely independent institutions of this sort, it would be harder to escape the pressures to conform to general societal standards or views.[7]

The decline in the independence of private associations is worrying from the point of view of liberty for another reason. Gray has very properly stressed the importance of what he calls a culture of liberty. The point is that mere rules or constitutional arrangements will not preserve liberty; in a society in which the appropriate traditions do not flourish, those rules will not be respected. Written constitutions do not hold society together; societies uphold their constitutions. One of the points writers in the classical liberal tradition have taken great pains to emphasise is that this requires of social institutions not merely a formal separation of powers among the various branches of government, but a wider distribution of power across society. This required, as Tocqueville in particular stressed, healthy private associations, independent of the state. Gray's insistence that governments 'tend and nurture' these intermediary institutions threatens to bring about their incorporation into the state, and the weakening of that separation of powers which is crucial to the preservation of individual liberty.

Conclusions

My remarks in this comment on John Gray's essay have generally been unremittingly critical—if not hostile! It may, by way of conclusion, be worth indicating why, especially since there are many points upon which we agree. Part of the reason is simply that criticism is usually more interesting than praise. But the more important reason has, I think, to do with the way in which Gray views his task as a political philosopher. While he has attempted to defend a principled philosophical position, he also makes it quite clear that he wants to confine philosophical discussion to the realm of policy possibilities. It is one of the 'postulates' of his argument that 'no modern state will in fact retreat to the sphere of minimum government' (p. 80). One of the reasons for his rejection of classical liberalism, I suspect, is that he sees such a philosophy as having no capacity to play a practical role in the real world of politics. Thus he is critical of classical liberal proposals for constitutional reform as naive (p. 86), and intimates that liberals are not cognisant of the complexity and the imperfectibility of human institutions.

I think Gray is probably right in his prognosis in the matter of the retreat of the state—it appears very unlikely.[8] This leads him to offer a principled defence of what he regards as a more attainable ideal outcome. To a classical liberal, I submit, the ideal he describes appears as a considerable improvement over the current state of things. The policies he proposes would, on his own estimate, mean a reduction of state expenditure to around a quarter of gross national product. While he complains that 'this transformation of government little short of revolutionary ... will not satisfy the fundamentalist advocates of *laissez faire*', this neglects the fact that it would still please them enormously. What the stubborn classical liberal does not want to do, however, is make a virtue out of a near-inevitability. Perhaps it is because, while Gray thinks that 'a genuine and lasting reduction in the size, cost and invasiveness of the state is to be achieved only by a revision and revaluation of the agenda of government in which its positive responsibilities are clearly and explicitly specified' (p. 89), classical liberals think it more important to uphold long-established principles—even if their prospects look bleaker than those of the fall of communism for the past seventy years.[9]

Notes

1   Raz also takes the view that autonomy requires that the individual possess the appropriate mental faculties, have available a range of worthwhile options, and not be subject to coercion. See *The Morality of Freedom*, p. 373.

2   Simon Leys, *Chinese Shadows*, New York: Viking Press, 1977, p. 194.

3   *Ibid.*, p. 194.

4   See Hayek, *Individualism and Economic Order*, Chicago: University of Chicago Press, 1948, pp. 112-13.

5   It is perhaps worth mentioning that the most significant segment of this bureaucracy is that part which deals with taxation. In Australia, its discretionary powers are growing daily; in the United States it considerably exceeds the size of the CIA and the FBI combined.

6   The problem of 'overuse' of medical services has led the Australian government to introduce, in August 1991 Budget, a $3.50 minimum charge for doctor's visits; in the same breath the government explained that the rising cost of Medicare was partly attributable to there being too many doctors in the system, and that measures would be taken to reduce numbers!

7   On current trends, one wonders, for example, how long before all 'private' associations are required to have a smoking policy—or, indeed, a no-smoking policy.

8   I think he is also right to say that the question is not a matter of the *size* of the state (p. 84).

9   My thanks to William Maley and David Lovell for comments on an earlier draft of this essay.

Gray on the Market*

Patrick Minford

John Gray, whose work I greatly admire, has produced a well-written and highly readable defence of the market on moral, as opposed to efficiency grounds. If I have criticisms, it is not that I disagree with the proposition that there is a moral case for the market; rather I believe that in making his particular moral case he has allowed in some strange and dangerous elements. There is much in his paper with which I agree: but naturally I focus on the rest.

His central argument is that free markets enable 'autonomy', whereas centrally planned socialist economies deny it. Autonomy however, which he defines as the wherewithal to pursue one's own concept of the good life, can also be prejudiced by the free play of market forces; unfortunate losers can be trampled underfoot. To remedy this prejudice, there should be a welfare system to ensure everyone's 'basic needs' are met; such needs he considers to be definable with reasonable objectivity and satiable (unlike 'positional' goods at the opposite extreme). 'Welfare rights' are introduced as short-hand for such a system; but Gray recognises there may be dangers in such language.

He goes on to criticise alternatives to his proposed welfare system. Negative income tax is a 'technical fix' that does not differentiate adequately between different needs. Swiss-style discretion is bureaucratic and demeaning. Egalitarianism is without moral justification and goes far further than required by

---

* In writing up these comments, I have benefited greatly from the lively discussion on the paper at the IEA, in particular comments by Dennis O'Keefe on vested interests, Shirley Letwin on autonomy and the author himself.

basic needs. Market socialism (worker cooperatives) is unworkable because it has no market in capital.

Finally, he describes some specific features of his welfare system. It would have the NHS—but stripped (how exactly without withdrawing free access?) of its redistribution to-and-from the middle classes ('churning'). There would be wide use of vouchers—e.g. for education—permitting a normal supply side of the market and entirely privately-financed demands co-existing with state-subsidised demands. Ordo-Liberal ideas would dictate the background of order and law required for the 'Social Market'. There would be a universal set of benefits, for unemployment, disability, community care, pensions, and so on, much as in the current post-Beveridge UK 'welfare state', available as of right according to central non-discretionary rules.

Let me begin with some specific doubts and queries.

Are there 'basic needs' which are satiable? The experience of the public spending debate fuelled by the present UK welfare system, which is not radically different from Gray's proposals, is that demands for the services of the NHS and education are in practice far from satiable. I understand perfectly the objective of ensuring a welfare 'safety net'; indeed I have described such an objective myself in my own proposals for dramatically limiting public spending. But if that is what Gray intends, he needs to be extremely careful in his description of the mechanisms that will limit the size of handouts (in the face of vocal vested interests), ensure that needs are met (as opposed to the goals of rent-seekers), and not destroy incentives. As it stands, his description sounds more like a recipe for Swedish-style welfarism, at vast cost to the average taxpayer (taxes in Sweden have now reached 58 per cent of GDP).

He gives little attention to incentives; indeed his rules are vague about such matters as means-testing (the rate of withdrawal?) and disqualification conditions (must someone look for a job to get unemployment benefit? Must an unmarried mother have no means of support to get single-parent benefit?). How do his proposals fail to create a Poverty Trap (far worse than that of the Negative Income Tax he reviles)? Does not the Swiss system of monitoring and local discretion not preserve incentives impressively? Could not charities, skilled in assessing genuine need, be involved more closely in the distribution of public charity?

Turning away from welfare to the defence of free markets, I am doubtful about Gray's lack of emphasis on economic efficiency (the economic 'Pareto-principle' whereby a larger cake can be realised to the benefit of all by suitable side-payments and bargaining). The collapse of centrally planned economies in Eastern Europe underlined this enormously strong case for capitalism. If free markets make most people better-off, and make it possible to improve the lot even of those who are worse off by modest transfers, then this is an unanswerable argument; only a bunch of sado-masochists would prefer the alternative. However sniffy one is about material measures like GNP, the fact remains that there are meaningful ways of identifying higher living standards for the mass of people and on such measures free market capitalism performs better by far than socialism. More refined arguments about the finer aspects of life capitalist societies lose (happy natives enjoying local customs in their primitive tribal state) are overturned by the vast migratory pressure into capitalist societies from those where these values are supposed to flourish. People want the living standards capitalism promotes and they want to combine them with the best from their own cultural values.

There is of course, as Gray urges, a moral case too. Free markets enable men to lead a free life. This is what I would understand by 'autonomy'. But Gray twists this word in a Rousseauesque way to mean 'the ability to enjoy the good life'; next he is prescribing redistributive taxation to enable all to enjoy the good life. There are two difficulties with his treatment.

First, there is the moral one: a man who is provided by others with the wherewithal to enjoy life thereby loses his autonomy in the usual sense, for he must submit to the decisions of others as to the conditions for provision.

Second, there are the incentives on which the success of capitalism depends. If you can have the good life anyway, why bother to work and strive?

Let me overlook a series of rather snide remarks about neo-liberals, Mrs Thatcher and President Reagan. Not everything in the 1980s was done right but it is far from clear that John Gray's suggestions, where they differ, represent any improvement. And it is ungenerous to ignore the massive advance in the cause of free markets—arguably bringing forward the collapse of Soviet planning—that was achieved in the 1980s.

The key claim made by Gray is that moral grounds are dominant because they underpin legitimacy. By the latter is meant that people submit readily to a set of social rules.

I would argue rather differently. Legitimacy occurs when a regime is not under serious threat from any major group in society. Such threats emerge when group interests are seriously compromised. These interests include not merely living standards according to usual measures but also freedom (autonomy in the usual sense) and other intangibles affecting the quality of life and, yes, moral approval. What is open to doubt is how powerful moral approval is as an independent force, as opposed to a rationalisation of other objectives. Was it moral approval that impelled C1 and C2 voters to swing to Mrs Thatcher in three elections? Was it morality that brought down the Soviet Union's centralised government—and not the collapse of the economy, after years of ineffective disgust at the Gulag? Was it morality that swung urbanised young Swedes' votes to the New Democrat free marketeers in September 1991?

Is not the legitimacy of the market founded on its ability to augment the cake and enhance freedom, so that all groups have an interest in seeing it prevail?

Societies discover by trial and error how far they can interfere with the market without generating serious group refusal. Britain for example experimented disastrously with high taxes on the rich, and temporarily lost the services of some of the most enterprising and talented; it also experimented with strong manual unions and incomes policies that ground down the skilled working classes, and lost again. History is full of similar and worse experiments. Surely legitimacy occurs when major group interests are satisfied; and morality then proceeds to hallow the result.

This approach suggests that the necessary transfer system to ensure the consent of the least well off will emerge from a bargain with the taxpaying majority. To achieve majority consent it may have to be a rather tougher and more hard-headed affair than John Gray describes, closer to Swiss Calvinism than to the open-handed universalism he espouses.

Autonomy, Social Rights and Distributive Justice

Raymond Plant

1. Over the fourteen years that I have known John Gray, I have learned a very great deal from him about the nature of liberalism, the role of markets and how to tackle some of the fundamental questions of political theory. He is one of the most consistently interesting political theorists writing today and unlike many others, perhaps including myself he has been prepared to change his mind on some essential issues, rather than continually trying to find new ways of defending old positions in which intellectual capital has been invested. The fact that I have not learned as much as he would have liked is shown by his critical assessment of my views on equality. Nevertheless over the years, the gap between us has narrowed. I have come to appreciate the case for market provision; he has come to appreciate the case for welfare rights which I have been arguing for some time, although we still differ about the scope of such rights and the extent to which they are subject to political bargaining. In this commentary I shall emphasise a number of points of remaining disagreement and where I think his argument needs further development.

2. I am sure that Gray is right to emphasise that both the intellectual and political case against command economies and central economic planning has been won. The intellectual debate since Reagan, Thatcher and the changes in Eastern Europe is really no longer about central economic planning or the case for the market but much more about the range of social and political institutions within which markets are embedded, the scope and purposes of these institutions, and their relationship to the market economy, along with the debate about the scope of the market and the range of goods which ought to be treated

as commodities. I believe that the case against central economic planning is at its most decisive on epistemological grounds and Gray's summary of the epistemic case against command economies as exemplified in the work of Hayek, Shackle and Polanyi is clear and masterly and one which I am prepared to accept. However, this is only part of the task of trying to work out the proper role for the market in a liberal society. This second task of trying to work out the appropriate moral limits to markets is also centrally important because the market is only likely to appear to be legitimate and command loyalty if it is seen to have a definite sphere of legitimacy and that it is constrained from spilling over into spheres of human life within which we do not wish to see goods treated as commodities. Given the degree of inequality which will naturally arise from free market exchange, and the fact that these will be influenced by morally arbitrary factors such as natural endowment, fortunate upbringing, and just sheer luck it is important to work out some consensual view about where appropriate limits lie for an institution which embodies these features.

3. Both Gray and I agree that autonomy is a basic need or interest of human beings, a view which I tried to set out in an abstract and philosophical way in *Political Philosophy and Social Welfare* (with H. Lesser and P. Taylor-Gooby, Routledge and Kegan Paul, 1981) and deployed in a more politically concerned way against negative liberty conceptions in *Conservative Capitalism in Britain and the United States: A Critical Appraisal* (with K. Hoover, 1989). However we still have some disagreement about the set of conditions necessary for the achievement of autonomy and I shall explore these a little in the commentary.

4. However, first of all I want to say something about the nature of autonomy as a political value. Since John Gray has also written a study called *A Conservative Disposition* which embodies an exploration of his own political standpoint it is presumably fair to call him a conservative and as someone who is likely to see the Conservative Party in the UK as the appropriate vehicle for the political achievement of the value of autonomy. However, it is important to recognise that many conservatives, both in the upper and lower case do not see autonomy as a conservative value at all. The best recent example of this known to me

is a very interesting pamphlet published by The Centre for Policy Studies called *The Conservative Community: The Roots of Thatcherism and Its Future* by Robin Harris sometime Director of the Research Department of the Conservative Party and Deputy Head of the Prime Minister's Policy Unit in Downing Street during the latter part of Mrs Thatcher's tenure of office. In this pamphlet Harris says things about the nature of conservatism which run directly counter to what Gray says about autonomy. There are several aspects to this disagreement which go to the heart of their different understandings of the nature of conservatism.

A. Gray argues in the present pamphlet for the inadequacy of negative liberty taken on its own. This is a view with which I agree and have argued for elsewhere (for example in *Equality Markets and the State*—the Fabian pamphlet which John Gray criticises later in the essay and in *Conservative Capitalism* cited above). We both agree that negative liberty understood as freedom from coercion cannot be a basic value on its own. To see why this might be thought to be so we might ask the defender of negative liberty why we want to be free from coercion? The most plausible answer to this question would be that when we are free from coercion we are then free to live a life shaped by our own values, purposes and plan of life. That is to say freedom from coercion is valuable to us because it is an indispensable condition for us to be able to live an autonomous life shaped by our own purposes and values. (As we shall see later, there is more at stake in the argument between negative and positive freedom and autonomy than this but for the moment let us stick with the view that negative liberty is valuable as a condition of autonomy and agency.) However consider what Harris says about this argument when he is criticising my view of it which, as I have said, on this point is exactly the same as Gray's:

> 'Freedom', (Professor Plant) writes, 'is valuable because it is a necessary condition of autonomy. But if this is why freedom is valuable, it cannot be separated from ability, resources and opportunities' ...the Conservative does not value freedom because of some other values; he values freedom in itself. The conservative has no ambition to be autonomous—were such a thing poss-

ible—indeed the prospect is one that he would find deeply disturbing.[1]

A similar argument is I think implicit in Lord Joseph and Jonathan Sumption's *Equality*, (John Murray, 1979).

However, we can already see two points of disagreement between Harris's conception of conservatism and that of Gray. The first is that for Harris, unlike for Gray and myself autonomy is not an ideal at all; secondly negative freedom is regarded both as the only defensible view of liberty and as being intrinsically valuable and not as a contribution to autonomy.

I am sure that Gray is on the stronger ground here because if freedom is valuable in itself then it just becomes a fundamental moral intuition, it is not regarded as contributing to a particular desirable sort of society nor to an ideal of human fulfilment and flourishing, namely an autonomous life. This considerably weakens the case for liberty, in that if someone disagreed about the importance or value of liberty understood in its negative sense, then all we could do would be to retreat to claiming its intuitive obviousness and not try to situate an account of why negative liberty is valuable in a wider account of human society and human flourishing. However, when there is just this conflict of basic intuitions between someone who intrinsically values negative liberty and someone who does not, then all we can do is to record the clash of intuitions, since if negative liberty is intrinsically valuable then there can be no further argument. This is hardly a strong position for a defender of liberal ideals of liberty to be in.

Nevertheless whatever the relative merits of Gray's position *vis a vis* Harris's there is still a fundamental clash about what constitutes the appropriate value basis of conservative thought (and practice).

B. Harris then goes on to criticise my claim, which is also to be found in Gray's current study that the sorts of resources that are necessary in both our view for the achievement of autonomy can be considered as rights. He writes as follows:

> The notion of citizenship involves opportunity, a set of needs, rights resources and opportunities which all individuals must have if they are to pursue any goals at all in our sort of society.

But who is to determine what these rights are. How can they be
fulfilled without the coercion of other individuals?[2]

Hence the claim that there are social and welfare rights based
upon an ideal of autonomy, a claim which forms a centre piece
of Gray's work, as well as mine which is what Harris is
criticising in this passage, is rejected as inconsistent with
conservative philosophy. (This view is consistent with Mrs
Thatcher's rejection of what she called 'The entitlement society'
in her book *Let Our Children Grow Tall*, Centre for Policy Studies,
1977.)

Hence to my mind there can be little doubt that in
emphasising the value of autonomy, the instrumentality of
negative liberty to autonomy, and the set of rights to go with it,
John Gray is challenging in a fundamental way Harris's
interpretation of the conservative disposition, not just in some
peripheral way, but at a central point.

5. I want now to turn back to the question of the nature of
liberty and its relation to autonomy. As I have already said, I
agree with the bulk of what Gray has said about liberty here,
but I want to make two additional points to strengthen the case
against conservative critics such as Harris as well as economic
liberals such as Hayek who want to draw a sharp distinction
between freedom, which in Hayek is understood as the absence
of intentional coercion, and ability and resources. If, as Gray and
I agree, autonomy is the central value to which negative
freedom makes a central contribution, then autonomy cannot be
separated from ability, resources and opportunities. While the
issue at stake here might be thought to be highly abstract and
rarefied, it is a point of quite central political importance. The
political issue at stake here has been rubbed in by both Hayek
and Keith Joseph from the standpoint of economic liberalism.
Hayek argues in *The Constitution of Liberty* that once liberty is
linked with ability (and the resources necessary to enable us to
do things) then there is at least a prima facie case for the
redistribution of resources from the rich to the poor in terms of
freedom in the sense that a limitation of ability is a limitation on
freedom, and that given the poor are less able to do things than
the rich, their freedom is limited. Hence the maintenance of a
separation of negative liberty from ability is central to block an

argument for the poor having a political claim on resources in the sense that their poverty is a limitation on their ability and hence an infringement of liberty. The political point is put very starkly by Keith Joseph and Sumption when they argue in *Equality* that 'Poverty is not unfreedom'. There might be, on this view, a case for welfare but this could not be cast in terms of an argument about liberty nor could it be based on the idea that people have a right to resources which they are unable to acquire through the market.

I have already considered one way of weakening this view which is to endorse John Gray's claim that once there is a recognition that negative freedom can only be justified in terms of the contribution that it makes to autonomy (if not why is liberty valuable to us?) then the claim that there is a sharp distinction to be drawn between being free to do something and being able to do it is not all that clear cut. We value negative liberty because it secures a sphere in which we are then able to do things. However if what makes liberty valuable is its link with what we are able to do, then we cannot sharply separate liberty and ability.

Nevertheless there are two other arguments which would strengthen this case which Gray does not mention. The first of these would be the claim that where there is no general ability to do something then freedom does not arise. If I asked whether or not people were able to write cheques in the thirteenth century we would, I think, be inclined to say that the question of freedom does not arise, since no one had the ability to write cheques. Because there was as yet no general ability to do this, any particular individual was neither free nor unfree to write cheques. However, if this is what one is inclined to say then we cannot draw a sharp distinction between freedom and ability. Indeed, the presence or absence of a generalised ability to do something could then be regarded as a necessary condition of being free or unfree to do it. If this is true then as a necessary condition of freedom, a general ability or capacity to do something cannot be separated from an analysis of freedom. Hence if there is a general capacity or ability in society, for example to eat in such a way as to secure physical health, and if I do not have the resources to do it, then *pace* Lord Joseph, poverty is unfreedom. Of course this leaves untouched the controversial question of how we are to understand poverty, but the main point remains true.

The second argument, which I owe to Charles Taylor goes as follows. If negative liberty is all there was to freedom, that is to say freedom is just the absence of coercion and is disconnected from any conception of the good whether held by individuals or society then how would we settle the question of whether one society is more free than another? The answer would surely lie in counting up the number of rules which limit freedom of action in the two societies whose degree of freedom we want to compare. That is to say it would have to be a quantitative judgement about the number of coercive rules which prevent action. It could not be a qualitative judgement about the importance of the rules in question—whether they limited important abilities since by definition freedom is assumed to be the absence of coercion, unconnected to an account either of abilities or to a conception of a social or individualised conception of the good. However, for the economic liberal or the conservative of Harris's persuasion this would lead to very paradoxical results. To take Charles Taylor's example: say we wanted to claim that Britain was a freer society that Albania. But what would this claim be based on? On the theory of negative liberty, it would have to be based on adding up the number of coercive rules. However, given that under the communists Albania was a fairly primitive society, for example with few traffic rules, whereas Britain as a highly mobile population with lots of traffic rules, then it might turn out to be the case that Albania has quantitatively fewer rules regulating conduct. However, this would surely be a very bizarre way of settling the issue of whether Albania was a freer society than the UK. We would surely be inclined to say that what matters in the judgement is a qualitative claim about what people in the UK are able to do that Albanians are not able to do—for example to criticise the government, to emigrate and so forth. That is to say, our judgement is based upon our view about a set of abilities and the way in which we value those abilities. In which case a pure theory of negative liberty is not crucial taken on its own or as an intrinsic value. It would have to depend on our conception of the good and the abilities which we think that people need in order to achieve what we regard as valuable in human life.

6. This leads us on to needs fairly naturally and this is a concept which looms quite large in Gray's argument for social rights.

The counter argument to the above would. be that while needs and abilities are crucial to the assessment of freedom and to conferring social rights (about which more below), nevertheless we lack a consensus about needs and abilities in a morally pluralistic society. This may lie behind Harris's under-developed criticism of this position when he says who will determine these rights, based upon a disputable concept of needs? So if we want to say as Gray does that social rights are defensible because they are based on those needs which are essential to autonomy which alone makes negative liberty valuable, do we have any way of arriving at a conception of needs which could be shared in a particular society as a basis for social rights, and thus for a shared conception of those needs which are necessary conditions for autonomy and freedom.

Before going on to discuss this point in detail, it is important to consider the economic liberal's critique of the idea of needs, since John Gray has in the past shared this critical standpoint in relation to needs. There are several interlocking aspects to the critique which can be found in the writings of economic liberals including John Gray in earlier writings as he himself acknowledges in the present study. The first is that in a morally pluralistic society we really have no way of arriving at a consensus over needs, these will differ between different moral communities within society. Or if there is a degree of consensus, the consensual list of needs will be so minimal that virtually any sort of government will satisfy this minimal list. So for example Gray himself once wrote as follows

> The objectivity of basic needs is equally delusive. Needs can be given no plausible cross-cultural content, but instead are seen to vary across different moral traditions. Even where moral traditions overlap so as to allow agreement to be reached on a list of basic needs, there is no means of arriving at an agreed schedule of urgency among conflicting basic needs. Again not all needs are in principle satiable. Think only of medical needs concerned with senescence. These are surely basic needs in that their non-satisfaction will result in death or worthless life... there is no natural limit on the resources that could be devoted to satisfying them. There

is an astonishing presumptuousness in those who write as if hard dilemmas of this sort can be subject to a morally consensual resolution. Their blindness to these difficulties can only be accounted for by their failing to take seriously the realities of cultural pluralism in our society; (or what comes to the same thing) to their taking as authoritative their own traditional values. One of the chief functions of the ideology of social justice may be, as Hayek intimates, to generate an illusion of moral agreement, where in fact there are profound divergencies of values.[3]

Most of the elements of the liberal critique are to be found in this passage: the vagueness and open-endedness of needs; the lack of a clear account of what would satisfy them and whether this is subject to a clear limit; disagreement in society over what needs actually are (and therefore the objectivity of any distinction between needs and preferences, wants and desires); the incommensurability of needs; and the fact (only implicit in this passage) that because of their vagueness and open-endedness interest group pressure can always expand the sphere of needs and thus the scope of government not to mention public expenditure.

Gray has now retracted some of this radical critique, but not all of it. So what is the crucial issue that has changed his mind. The answer lies in his adherence to the view set out by Joseph Raz in *The Morality of Freedom* that there is a class of definable satiable needs and that this can then be used as a basis for a society to confer social rights in respect of such limited needs. This is what Gray now in the present study argues, following Raz:

> Raz illuminates a fundamental property of basic needs, as distinct from wants or preferences, when he notes that they are, most of them, in principle capable of complete satiation. The needs of the disabled or the illiterate, though sometimes expensive to meet can be met completely, that is to say to the point at which they can lead reasonably autonomous lives... Most basic needs have the property of satiability, which means that, once they are met, the content of the welfare right which guarantees their satisfaction, is exhausted.

There is no doubt in my mind that this argument is central to Gray's thesis both in terms of meeting the economic liberal's critique of social rights while at the same time distinguishing his position from both social democracy and socialism which would take a more redistributive view of social rights. If Raz's principle is well grounded, then it would be absolutely central to meeting the economic liberal's critique of needs based welfare rights, in the sense that (*pace* the economic liberal) needs would be satiable rather than openended and the obligations and resources to which these needs would give rise would be clear and limited. It is also central to distinguishing his position from those further to the Left in that if most needs are satiable, then they do not have a tendency to grow and thus this would put a clear limit on the extent to which they are to be seen as redistributive.

However, as it stands the argument seems to me to be under-developed and the lacunae in the argument could turn out to be quite crucial in the argument with the economic liberal and in distinguishing his argument from a social democratic or socialist one. There are clearly some aspects of the Raz/Gray case which give cause for worry. As Gray himself says in the above passage most of the set of basic needs are in principle capable of satiation. This claim is a bit vague. Which are satiable and which are not and what lies behind the idea of a need being in principle satiable?

Secondly, as Gray again notes, the principle of satiation for him means the capacity to lead a reasonably autonomous life. What is to be the test of this?: the self avowal of the individual, that his need satisfaction has now reached a level where the degree of his or her autonomy cannot be increased; expert judgement—doctors, teachers, social workers, welfare adminis-trators/managers of various sorts; or political judgement, based upon some degree of consensus (of the sort that Gray earlier denied) about what would be a reasonable level to meet such needs and thus the conditions of autonomy. It seems that in some sense the issue of vagueness has been transferred from needs to autonomy and what constitutes a reasonable level of autonomy these issues are vital to the coherence of Gray's argument partly to distance his new position from the economic liberal critique which he once accepted, and partly to differentiate it from a social democratic or socialist conception of welfare rights. He wants to argue that this latter position is involved in seeing social rights as connected with social or distributive justice and doing this partly by trading upon the open-endedness of needs. Since more can always be done to increase need satisfaction through social rights, social rights would then become an instrument for achieving greater social justice and greater social and economic equality. Gray wants to distinguish his position very clearly from this and the idea that needs do have natural limits of satiability is the crucial element in this attempt to differentiate his more restrictive view of welfare rights and the needs on which they rest from a more expansive, redistributive and egalitarian socialist or social democratic one.

However, it does seem to me that for so crucial a principle in the argument more work needs to be done on it before it is really plausible because Gray's own formulation of it in the present study (in the passage cited above) is rather qualified. As he himself subsequently makes clear the argument about the principled satiability of needs does not apply to health needs which mirrors his more sceptical argument from his earlier more committed economic liberal period as demonstrated in the passage quoted earlier. Excluding health from the class of satiable needs, but still regarding this area of need as conferring rights, is a rather large exception. Undoubtedly, as he says, health may pose a problem for any theory (or more accurately for any theory of a non-libertarian sort—the libertarian who does not recognise an obligation to meet needs would say that health needs must be self defined and fulfilled in a market context). But it is such a large exception that it does weaken his argument in respect of social democratic/socialist theories of needs and welfare rights because as I have said it is crucial to his own case for differentiating his own position from a more redistributive one that there is such a class of basic satiable needs underpinning welfare rights.

My own view of this is that Gray is correct in saying that there is a class of needs the satisfaction of which is a necessary condition for autonomy, but I am not at all convinced by his argument developed here that such needs are clearly satiable and therefore the welfare rights connected with them clearly circumscribed by the condition of satiability. I think that the limitations on need satisfaction and thus the content of social rights is more likely to be found in the idea that we have to try for a consensus in respect of what we regard as meeting such needs, recognising the fact that there are clearly resource limitations. This consensus will have to be subject to continuous political negotiation, but against the background of resource constraints is going to include the idea of fairness. If not all needs are satiable then the content of welfare rights will have to be negotiated in a way that embodies some conception of what a fair degree of provision for a particular set of rights is going to be. Instead of the limit to provision being set by, as it were, an internal conception of satiation, it will have to be settled by a negotiation of what we regard as fair provision in a particular society against a background of limited resources. However, this necessarily links up the idea of social or welfare rights with the distributive notion of fairness which Gray wants to avoid. It also links it to the idea of a fair value for liberty defended by John Rawls in *A Theory of Justice*. If welfare rights and the needs that underpin them are necessary conditions of autonomy as Rawls, Gray and myself argue, and if the goal of a liberal political order is securing the basis of autonomy for all citizens, then either these conditions are limited by the fact of satiability as in Gray, or by distributive fairness as in Rawls' conception. Thus if the argument about the satiability of needs cannot be made, then it does seem to me that Gray's argument will turn into the distributive one which he wants to avoid and is the main principle which distinguishes his view from a social democratic one.

So, for example, health care: a start might be made by trying to achieve some kind of consensus about a set of core health services which any health authority should be required to provide as rights (which would also imply rights to standards of delivery, waiting times etc.) with other services being discretionary or being paid for. The needs may not be clearly satiable but I see no reason why we cannot achieve some degree of consensus which will define a set of rights or entitlements which should prevail given that consensus about what constitutes a fair distribution of resources for health within the limits of public expenditure. Despite a lot of political differences, we have had such a consensus in the case of education. The needs are not necessarily satiable, but we can, I think, achieve a broad consensus so long as all parties are prepared to acknowledge the fact of scarcity and that needs will outrun resources and this consensus will have to involve some appeal to distributive justice in a way which Gray regards as objectionable. On the Rawlsian view therefore welfare rights are inextricably connected with distributive justice in that the resources allocated to satisfy such rights as conditions of autonomy will have to make reference to some distributive conceptions as a way of producing a fair distribution of the means to autonomy or more briefly in terms of Rawls' idea of the fair value of liberty. One reason why governments have fallen victim to interest group pressures in relation to services to satisfy needs is that they have been unwilling to face the fact of scarcity and attempt to try to construct some degree of agreement about what would at a particular time be a reasonable degree of entitlement given limited resources. This seems to me to be a more realistic approach than assuming that there is clearly a class of satiable needs which will then specify the limit of resource provision to meet the rights which depend upon these limited needs. In my view the weight has to be put on a negotiated political consensus rather than on the idea that a range of needs is clearly satiable in terms of a reasonable level of autonomy. The idea of a reasonable level of autonomy will enter into the political negotiation, but I do not believe that there is a limit to the satisfaction of the need to be derived from the satiability principle which makes it in some sense circumscribed and independent of political and interest group pressure.

It should also be remembered, for reasons on which Gray and I agree and which will be rehearsed in the next section, that exactly the same set of questions arise in relation to the needs which underlie what might be called negative rights not to be interfered with in ways proscribed by such rights. These rights will involve public expenditure to protect them in the way of police forces and other security-promoting forms of public expenditure. Are these needs, such as the need for physical security, to be regarded as limited by the notion of satiability, or are we back again with distributive justice and the need to negotiate a fair distribution of resource allocation to protect negative rights?

7. I believe that Gray is absolutely correct to argue that there is no sharp distinction between civil and political rights and welfare rights, and I have used similar arguments to try to establish the same point within a position to the left of John Gray's.[4] To some extent the position mirrors the debate about negative and positive liberty. If rights are supposed to protect liberty and to impose obligations on others in terms of respecting my freedom, then if what grounds the importance of negative liberty is autonomy and that in turn implies both freedom from coercion and access to resources, the rights to protect liberty will be both negative (to protect me from coercion) and positive (to guarantee me access to resources—a guarantee which cannot be secured within the market). However, the argument can be strengthened compared with Gray's own version of the symmetry of negative and positive rights.

If we have a right to the protection of negative rights, then this implies the commitment of resources to this protection eg. police forces, courts etc. Therefore, the distinction between negative and positive rights cannot be cast in terms of the former being achievable without resources in that the corresponding obligation is the costless one of abstaining from coercion. If we were a community of saints who always forbore to interfere then this might be true, but in the real world the obligation to forebear from coercion, interference, assault etc. has to be forced on those who are not inclined to forebear and this is not going to be a costless exercise. This is the force of Gray's own argument. However, it can be taken one stage further in terms of the idea that there must be a right to this protection of civil and political or negative rights. The reason for this is that rights have to be enforceable if they are to be rights at all. It is the legitimate enforceability and thus a right to the protection of such rights that counts and this will be a positive right to the enforcement of rights and thus will necessarily involve both costs and resources.

Hence, those who have wanted to distinguish between negative rights (typically civil and political rights) and positive rights (typically welfare rights) in terms of the costless nature of the former and the resource implications of the latter are mistaken. In order to explain why negative rights should be seen as rights as opposed to other sorts of claims, then they have to be enforced and yet the right to have my rights protected is a positive right implying resources.

8. Gray spends a little time on the question of whether or not some of the welfare rights he does want to defend should be linked to obligations of a workfare or learnfare type. That is to say that they should not in some cases, for example unemployment benefits for the able bodied be regarded as unconditional rights of citizenship, but rather as conditional on being prepared to work perhaps in government-funded schemes, in which the government is, so to speak, the employer of last resort, or at least to engage in training programmes of various sorts. I have very mixed feelings about this argument and find it genuinely hard to make up my mind. Having defended workfare as a possibility in *Citizenship, Rights and Socialism*, the Fabian pamphlet to which Gray refers, I have had some second thoughts. It is therefore worth just looking in more detail at the arguments than Gray does in his study.

The first argument in favour of workfare is that a right to a resource does not enhance autonomy unless in some sense the resources have come to an individual through his or her own efforts. This argument has been best stated by an American political theorist Donald Moon from what in Britain we would call a social democratic perspective. Hence it would be a mistake to think that the idea of workfare is essentially a right-wing argument. This is what Moon says:

> The entire approach of analysing the welfare state simply in terms of a human right to welfare is mistaken. Even if we could show that we have such rights, this approach would not solve the problem that Hegel diagnosed, because providing relief for those in need, even when they have a right to it, may nevertheless still cause them to lose status and self respect.

He then goes on to link the idea of self respect with living up to the norms and values implicit in a particular society and he goes on to argue that in American society, if one is able bodied, then this means living an independent life which he then goes on to link with autonomy in the following way:

The expectation of independence is grounded in our understanding of ourselves as morally equal, autonomous agents, whose relationships are governed in part by the norm of reciprocity. In the context of civil society, dependence of one person on another violates the ideal of reciprocity. Often such dependence involves relationships of moral inequality, premised on the subordination of one person to another. But even when subordination is absent, the dependent person receives something without offering anything in return. As Hegel put it, for people to receive their subsistence from the state 'directly, not by means of their work, ... would violate the principle of civil society and the feeling of individual independence and self respect in its individual members'.[5]

Moon concludes from this that an unconditional set of welfare rights might well undermine the very sense of autonomy and self respect that welfare rights were supposed to underpin and on this basis workfare/learnfare might have moral legitimacy in terms of the fundamental value of autonomy.

The second argument is that it is just not conceivable within a basically capitalist society that people can in any event be convinced that they have rights to resources which they have not in fact earned. The dominant idiom of capitalism is that the resources that I can command arise through contract and through my own efforts. The idea of welfare states, for the reasons stated by Hegel in *The Philosophy of Right*, in fact violate this principle of capitalist civil society. The point has been put in modern terms by Robert Pinker

The idea of paying through taxes or holding authentic claims by virtue of citizenship remains largely an intellectual conceit of the social scientist and the socialist. For the majority the idea of participant citizenship in distributive processes outside the market place has very little meaning. Consequently most applicants for social services remain paupers at heart.[6]

The third argument is more pragmatic although it does draw some inspiration from the other two and it seems to be the one which Gray adopts, namely that making benefits, particularly unemployment benefits conditional on discharging obligations in the work place or the training place may be in the interests of the unemployed themselves. Without obligations they become privatised and dependent. They lose skills and the disciplines of the labour market.

What are we to make of these arguments? As I said earlier I find it difficult to make up my mind and all that I can do is to rehearse the counter arguments to those above.

If it is thought that unconditional rights create dependency and a lack of self esteem, then it does not follow that workfare is the best answer. If jobs are to be provided by government or at least funded by government, then these are not like jobs acquired in the normal labour market, but are forms of make-work which the unemployed are, as it were, slotted into rather than earning from their own efforts. It is not clear that this will enhance independence, and it is at least arguable that if it does not, then the fact of dependency (if it is a fact) is being transferred from the Department of Social Security to the Department of Employment. In addition, it would presumably cost quite a lot more than unemployment benefit. This would be for two reasons. First of all, if in some sense genuine work is being done and products sold, then both the products and the rates of return to labour are likely to be higher than the current levels of unemployment benefit. Secondly, such work will have to be organised and this will involve either government directly organising it, or alternatively funding others to do so. In either case, this is likely to be more expensive than just paying unemployment benefit through an existing bureaucratic system. Thus the public expenditure implications of such an approach would be horrendous.

However, Gray seems to be arguing much more for learnfare and training as the appropriate obligation. Here the crucial issue, seems to be the likelihood of returning to a level of employment such as has been the historical experience of western societies since the war and up to the mid 1970s. If one is convinced that there is a good prospect of full employment (subject to non-accelerating inflation rate of unemployment) and that there will be jobs for trained people, that is to say people who have trained as part of their learnfare obligation, then there might be good reasons to go down the learnfare road. However, if one believes this not to be realistic then learnfare could turn out to be rather cruel unless there were jobs to be filled. Only if we return to the idea of government being the employer of last resort would this problem then be solved. Then the problem for Gray would be this. Given that he thinks that limited government and thus limited public expenditure and limited government involvement in the labour market is a good thing, then the government being the employer of last resort would consort rather unhappily with these assumptions and it would be better to pay benefits as a right rather than in a conditional way when the circumstances in which the conditional obligations could be discharged might well run counter to other aspects of his economic liberalism. So in my view a lot will depend upon one's assumptions about the future of employment.

There is however a deeper philosophical issue at stake here. The conditional approach to welfare rights for the able bodied requires them to discharge a concomitant obligation as we have seen. However, we do not make civil and political rights contingent on leading a virtuous life except in the limited sense of criminals losing the right to vote. Workfare and learnfare programmes defended on the basis that Donald Moon indicates, however, link such welfare rights to living a virtuous life, that is, living in accordance with dominant conceptions of autonomy, self reliance and independence. If, as Gray and I agree, there is no clear categorical difference between welfare rights and civil and political rights, then it is unclear on what kind of principle welfare rights are being made conditional on virtue being shown while civil and political rights are not (subject to the minimal restriction in the case of criminals mentioned above). Is the willingness to entertain a conditional basis for welfare rights perhaps symptomatic of an assumption that these are not in fact genuine rights? However, all of Gray's arguments in this study suggest that there is not a difference of principle between them. It is largely because I believe that there is no way of distinguishing them, that I am more inclined than I was to think that they should not be ascribed on a conditional basis, any more than civil and political rights are.

9. I now want to turn to Gray's strictures on my own more distributive approach to the issues of welfare rights. The basis of my defence of my position has already been laid in my earlier scepticism about the satiability of need argument. If Gray is not able to limit needs by the satiability constraint, then it does seem to me that issues of needs, welfare rights and some

conception of fairness and social justice come together. If needs cannot be internally constrained by satiability, then the only solution for someone who believes in the salience of needs for politics is to say that the welfare right based on needs is a right to a fair or a just share of social resources to meet such needs and that, as I have said, this judgement has to be arrived at in terms both of a recognition of the importance of fairness and justice, but also a recognition of the inherent scarcity of resources. Hence I am basically unrepentant about my own concern for distributive justice which in *Equality Markets and the State*, (the main object of Gray's attack) was linked to the Rawlsian idea of securing a fair value for liberty by securing to people rights to resources which they could not get or at least could not guarantee getting in the market. And that this distributive concern is linked to autonomy in the sense that if the satisfaction of welfare needs is a necessary condition for autonomy, and if such needs cannot be constrained by internal satiability, then the fair value of liberty has to be involved in distributive questions. Having said this, it still seems to me that something like Rawls' difference principle, that social and economic inequalities are justified if they are to the advantage of the least advantaged which was the conception of justice defended in *Equality Markets and the State*, is still the most defensible distributive principle which remedies the defects of procedural equality of opportunity, without embodying all the defects of equality of outcome. However, I repeat the point that distributive justice seems to me to be a central issue if needs are not to be regarded as satiable in the rather vague way (and subject to large exceptions) that Gray and Raz propose. I do however want to turn to one or two of the specific strictures that Gray makes of the position outlined in *Equality Markets and the State*.

Gray argues that I have a defective view of empowerment in which empowerment is seen as having a necessarily distributive dimension. I argued that this was the case because power is a positional good in that it declines in value the more widely it is distributed and disappears altogether if it is distributed equally. In my view therefore empowerment has to be concerned with distribution and that in crucial respects empowerment is a zero sum business, with individuals being empowered only by transferring power from other individuals or groups. In the study I did argue that for very many goods the market was the very best mechanism for their distribution, and that clearly not all goods are positional, and that the market can cope perfectly properly with these sorts of goods (for the reasons which Gray has so admirably set out in Chapter 2 of his study) better than any other system. However, I did argue that for some sorts of goods empowerment is positional and can be achieved only by disempowering others. On this crucial issue at stake between us Gray says the following:

> The conceptual fallacy in Plant's argument is in assimilating the empowerment of the poor and needy to the model of political power. Empowerment, or better, enablement, as I understand it, means conferring on such people the opportunities and resources they need to live autonomously. It is thoroughly unclear, and Plant gives us no reason to suppose, that the enablement of any person necessarily, or even commonly, entails the disablement of any other. How do welfare benefits for the disabled, perhaps framed in terms of voucher schemes, limit or disempower the able bodied? In general, such schemes will have the effect of enhancing autonomy in the population, without incurring any cost in the heteronomy of others. Because it is a satiable good, autonomy—the basis of many of the welfare benefits that are defended here—is rarely if ever a positional good.

There are several issues at stake in this argument which need to be treated carefully. The distinction between empowerment and enablement is crucial since Gray does accept that power is a pure form of a positional good, and he is right to think that my more distributive argument trades on that assumption. However, as he claims in the passage the distinction does trade on the assumption that needs are satiable, and as I have suggested this principle, while crucial to Gray's argument at many places is vague, and, as he admits, is subject to some central exceptions. Nevertheless it is crucial to the distinction which he then uses against my argument. The satisfaction of needs through welfare rights is enablement for Gray because such rights are subject to clear constraints in terms of the satiability of the needs in question. It is this claim, however, that has to be defended more fully than Gray does in this study.

There is however, an additional argument in favour of my position the grounds of which I believe are to be found in the passage just cited. Part of Gray's argument for thinking that social rights or entitlements enhance autonomy is that they do give greater power to the person bearing the rights in respect of professional administrators of welfare and social resources. This has certainly been part of the liberal case for vouchers that Gray himself cites in the passage just quoted. On the public choice view of the behaviour of public sector bureaucracies, vouchers are a way of empowering the recipient of the voucher, but not just in the sense of enablement, but rather empowering the bearer of the entitlement or the voucher against the public sector official who might otherwise determine the nature, the terms and the level of the service offered according to the professional discretion of the official, whether social security official, consultant, G.P., teacher, social worker or whatever. This seems much closer to my view of empowerment as a positional good than Gray's view about enablement which disempowers or disables no one else.

It seems to me that conferring rights, entitlements, or vouchers and the whole movement in respect of citizen's charters—now popular across the political spectrum, and a case which I argued in the IEA study *Citizenship and Rights in Thatcher's Britain*, is essentially about empowering the citizen, the consumer, the patient, the parent, the client against professional groups in the public sector. It is not about some limited level of enablement which leaves power relations intact. It is rather about the redistribution of power from professional groups to the consumer of professional services outside the market sector. Hence, in my view social rights and entitlements would in fact be essentially redistributive because such rights are involved in redistributing power.

Take Gray's own example of vouchers for the disabled. In giving this choice-enhancing measure to individuals, it seems to me that the power of professionals who are in charge of resources and services for the disabled would be diminished. It may be true as Gray says that resources for the disabled may not limit or disempower the able bodied but that is surely not the point. The people from whom the power is being redistributed is the professional group in question. Hence, I believe that the empowerment of the poor and needy through rights and entitlements is essentially redistributive, that this power is a positional good and what is at stake is a zero sum game in that the power of the needy enhanced through rights is at the expense of others, not to be sure the general group of the able bodied, but rather the professional groups with responsibilities in this area.

To sum up then: my concern with distributive issues in general reflects my general sense of being unconvinced by the Raz/Gray argument about the satiability of need. If needs are not satiable then we have to be in the business of figuring out the degree of fairness in the allocation of resources to meet such needs since both Gray and I agree these have to ·be achieved through rights rather than through the market. Secondly, as I have just said, once we are in the business of satisfying basic needs through rights in the public sector, then conferring rights is a zero sum or distributive business and is involved in a systematic disempowering of producer interests in the public sector.

I shall leave my response to Gray's fine study on this point. He goes on to criticise market socialism, but I am not in this sense a market socialist. Indeed in a Fabian pamphlet, *Market Socialism: Whose Choice?*[7] it was pointed out by Forbes, the editor, that the authors of that pamphlet had reacted against my earlier *Equality Markets and the State* and I made my position *vis a vis* market socialism clear in my contribution to *Market Socialism.*[8] The theorists who defend market socialism against Gray can do so more effectively than I can as a non-subscriber to their view. I should emphasise that despite the fact that Gray and I still disagree, his study has certainly given me a great deal of food for thought and has imposed on me a need to re-examine my own views, as he has been scrupulous in developing his own.

Notes

1   Robin Harris, *The Conservative Community: The Roots of Thatcherism and Its Future*, London: Centre for Policy Studies, 1989, p. 29.

2   *Loc. cit.*

3   John Gray, 'Classical Liberalism and the Politicisation of Poverty' in *Dilemmas of Liberal Democracies*, (ed) A. Ellis and K. Kumar, Tavistock, 1983, p. 182.

4   See 'Needs, Agency and Welfare Rights', in (ed) D. Moon, *Responsibility, Rights and Welfare*, Westview Press, 1988.

5   D. Moon, 'The Moral Basis of The Welfare State', in (ed) A. Gutmann, *Democracy and the Welfare State*, Princeton, 1988.

6   R. Pinker, *Social Theory and Social Policy*, Heinemann, 1971, p. 142.

7   *Market Socialism: Whose Choice?*, (ed) I. Forbes, Fabian Society, 1985.

8   *Market Socialism*, (eds) J. Le Grand and S. Estrin, Clarendon Press, 1989.

Suggestions for Further Reading

Undergraduate

Will Kymlicka, *Contemporary Political Philosophy: an Introduction*, Oxford: Clarendon Press, 1990.

Raymond Plant, *Modern Political Thought*, Oxford: Blackwell, 1991.

Norman Barry, *Introduction to Modern Political Theory*, 2nd Edition, London: Macmillan, 1989.

Postgraduate

J. Raz, *The Morality of Freedom*, Oxford: Clarendon Press, 1986.

I. Berlin, *Four Essays on Liberty*, Oxford: Oxford University Press, 1969.

J. Feinberg, *Social Philosophy*, New Jersey: Prentice Hall, 1973.

Sam Brittan, *Capitalism and the Permissive Society*, London: Macmillan, 1973.

Recent Health and Welfare Unit Publications

1992 and the Regulation of the Pharmaceutical Industry
April 1990, £6.95. ISBN 0-255 36259-5

MIKE L. BURSTALL

Dr Burstall's study of the regulation of the pharmaceutical industry by the EC considers the pros and cons of national as opposed to European regulation. Among the issues he examines are price and profit regulation, patent law and product licensing on grounds of both safety and efficacy, each of which holds lessons for other industries which trade in Europe.

The Emerging British Underclass
May 1990, £5.95. ISBN 0-255 36263-3

CHARLES MURRAY, *Manhattan Institute for Policy Research*
FRANK FIELD, *Labour Member of Parliament for Birkenhead, Chairman of the Social Services Select Committee*
JOAN C. BROWN, *Independent Researcher in Social Policy*
ALAN WALKER, *Professor of Social Policy, University of Sheffield*
NICHOLAS DEAKIN, *Professor of Social Policy and Administration, University of Birmingham*

'Britain has a small but growing underclass of poor people cut off from the values of the rest of society and prone to violent, anti-social behaviour, according to a report published today by the Institute of Economic Affairs.' *The Times*

'Mr Murray ... cites three early-warning signs from the US — rising illegitimacy, violent crime, and refusal to work — which are increasing in Britain.' *The Daily Telegraph*

Equalizing People
July 1990, £3.95. ISBN 0-255 36262-5

DAVID G. GREEN, Director, *IEA Health and Welfare Unit*

'The IEA ... is gearing up for another crusade.' *Financial Times*

Morality, Capitalism and Democracy
September 1990, £3.95. ISBN 0-255 36266-8

MICHAEL NOVAK, *American Enterprise Institute*

'A leading American intellectual ... with the message that capitalism is not simply a successful ideology; it can also capture the moral high-ground. Professor Novak's aim is to produce a set of ideals by which democratic capitalist societies may judge themselves.'

The Independent

Other Health and Welfare Unit Publications

The Spirit of Democratic Capitalism

Feb. 1991, £12.95. 463pp. ISBN 0-8191-7823-3

PROFESSOR MICHAEL NOVAK

'Michael Novak ... has done us a service in illuminating where the fault lines between right and left now lie.'　　　　Will Hutton, *Guardian*

'Mr Major ... might seek inspiration from *The Spirit of Democratic Capitalism* ... There is much to be gained from a skip through.'
　　　　Joe Rogaly, *Financial Times*

Empowering the Elderly

May 1991, £6.95. 50pp. ISBN 0-255 36268-4

WILLIAM LAING

'Vulnerable and dependent people are not well served by monopolies which make discretionary decisions on their behalf', according to economist William Laing.

Is British Food Bad for You?

June 1991, £4.95. 36pp. ISBN 0-255 36267-6

PROFESSOR VINCENT MARKS

'A leading nutritionist makes a scathing attack on "food terrorists" who spread unscientific scare stories about so-called health foods.'
　　　　Independent

'Fad eating is the greatest food health risk in Britain ... warns leading biochemist.'　　　　*London Evening Standard*

Saving Lives

Sept. 1991, £5.95. 34pp. ISBN 0-255 36269-2

P. BASKETT, M. IRVING, B. MCKIBBIN & R. MURLEY

'More than 1,000 people die every year in Britain because of the failure of accident and emergency services, according to a report published today.'　　　　*The Times*